TRANSSEXUAL

ALL DIFFERENT,
ALL HUMAN

Based on real facts, people,
and entities.

Carlos Marques

"It's much easier when you understand that it's not necessary to agree. You just need to accept different points of view."
— Suely Buriasco

"If you don't respect differences, you will never discover similarities."
— Verônica Clow

"Wisdom consists in knowing how to listen and respecting the differences of others."
— Damião Maximino

"It doesn't matter what you think, if you don't respect differences. You'll always believe you hold the truth, even if it's a lie."
— Óscar Klemz

PREAMBLE

I have always been motivated by the causes of oppressed minorities, likely because, from a young age, I began to admire those who, in clandestine minorities, fought against established powers.

It was then that I allowed myself to be swept up in a naïve youthful romanticism, inspired by the struggle of the French Resistance against Nazi rule, and later, by the fight that a minority in Portugal waged against the Estado Novo dictatorship.

In this way, I developed a political and social awareness that ideologically placed me on the side of the weaker, without any intention of becoming condescending, much less paternalistic.

I do not consider myself indoctrinated, either by a gospel or by any political dogma. I am not affiliated with any club or political party. It seems to me the only way to remain independent.

The fictional stories I write are set against a backdrop of social critique, humanist, independent, and non partisan, free from creeds or ideological disciplines.

For my readers, it has likely not gone unnoticed that behind each mundane story, there is always a denunciation or critique of a particular social reality that forms the setting for the narrative.

In several poems from *METEORS*, it was the experience of living with someone suffering from manic-depressive psychosis that dictated the rebellion of words and the disillusionment of feelings.

In *PEOPLE WITHOUT HOPE*, it was the denunciation of Ceausescu's dictatorship in communist Romania.

In *THEY DO NOT GOVERN OR ALLOW TO BE GOVERNED*, heavily laden with political denunciation, I tried to paint a social portrait of Portugal from the fall of the monarchy in 1910 to the 25th of April 1974 revolution.

... and MAN created god is a cry denouncing religious dogmas and the liberation of an avowed atheist.

In *VASE WITH BLUE FLOWERS*, beyond the story, there are problems related to the theft and forgery of works of art.

In *THE PHOTOGRAPHER'S LOOK*, although it is a book about photography, I did not fail to weave a sharp and blunt critique of the speculation that pervades much of what is called Contemporary Art, challenging the pseudo-intellectualism that dominates it.

In *EUROPE'S SUICIDE*, while defending multiculturalism and human solidarity with refugees and their social integration, there is also a denunciation of the progressive Islamisation of Europe, without any control, the loss of European identity, and the associated security risks.

In *WAR GAMES*, the entire story revolves around one of today's key issues: internet insecurity, crime on the Dark Web, criminal hackers, and the ethical hackers working for justice.

In *THE SECRET MUSEUM*, in addition to exposing corruption and the fraudulent origins of vast multimillion-dollar fortunes, particularly among Russian oligarchs, I return to the problem of art theft, the forgery of artworks, and the trafficking of archaeological antiquities.

My tenth book, *AI ART*, has nothing to do with social critique or ideological positioning. It is a book about art specifically, digital painting based on original photographs taken by me.

For my 11th book, *TRANSSEXUAL - ALL DIFFERENT, ALL HUMAN*, I took some time to decide on a subject often considered taboo, a controversial and poorly understood, though fiercely criticised, regarding what are wrongly called LGBT sexual disorders.

After an initial round of internet research on the topic, particularly regarding the transgender community, the information I gathered was deeply alarming in terms of the intolerance they face and the attacks they endure from society. When I learned that the average life expectancy of a transgender person in Brazil is just 35 years, due to being denied access to any profession, leaving prostitution as their only option, where they are often tortured, murdered, or driven to suicide, I initially found the topic too violent and depressing to pursue.

However, on further reflection, I felt that precisely because of these reasons, I should do something within the very limited scope of my abilities, to at least raise awareness, denounce the situation, and encourage readers, ordinary people like me, to try to understand the causes and motivations of these individuals.

What is typically observed on this issue is a superficial, malicious, and slanderous perspective from those on the outside who harshly criticise those within, often driven more by ancestral beliefs than by true knowledge or rationality. The preference is to maintain the issue as a taboo and relegate these outcasts to an impenetrable form of apartheid.

But careful observation of current events highlights the hypocrisy of a society that is intolerant yet secretly permissive and promiscuous. Just look at the number of advertisements for transvestites in the "Conviviality" section of *Correio da Manhã newspaper*, or on specialised websites, which offer a vast showcase of what the market has to offer. If there are many of these advertisements, it's because there are clients, possibly the very same people who publicly condemn them to ostracism in order to camouflage their own tendencies.

I have therefore decided to take on what may be the greatest challenge of my brief career as a writer. I intend to venture into this taboo area, a world completely unknown to the majority, a ghetto that, like any other, is inhabited by human beings who, no matter how misunderstood, deserve respect.

My aim is to do a work that emphasises humanism and the attempt to understand life choices that are difficult for most to grasp. There is always more than one perspective to approach any aspect of life. I will approach this work from a standpoint of respect for differences and their acceptance, as opposed to the usual narrative surrounding this issue, which tends to focus on intolerance, destructive criticism, and slander.

BRAZIL

1999

Parintins. Amazon River

In the late afternoon, after a dawn and morning of fishing and the subsequent sale of what remained beyond the household's needs, on the streets of Parintins, the riverside fishermen of the small Amazonian town, gather informally at Tadeu's bar for a chat and to savour the tingling sensation in their mouths caused by the jambu cachaça.

In the absence of any professional or social association, the place is frequented by the residents of the São José Operário neighbourhood, squeezed between the Amazon River and Macurany Lake. They are the poorest in Parintins, descendants of indigenous people, fishermen, caboclos, riverside dwellers, small farmers, and rubber tappers, all of them products of a fusion of various cultures and ethnicities over the centuries.

The oldest, Seu Joacir, so distinguished by the respect his white beard and advanced age have earned him, speaks like a priest from the pulpit:

- Since I was five or six years old, I went to see my father fishing. Being the son of a fisherman, I love it, love it! For me, there's nothing else but fishing. It's where I earn my living... Fishing, to me, is everything. When I was born, what my father and mother taught me was this, and for me, it's a source of pride to be a fisherman. The more I do it, the more I love my profession. The more I pull in fish, the prouder I am, because I was born into this and am the son of a fisherman who also took pride in spearing pirarucu. Back then, there were plenty of them.

The listeners pay close attention because he speaks about everything that matters to them, sharing in the hardship of their lives.

- Back in the day, in Parananema, we didn't have the heavy gear we have now: trawlers, big nets. Why the big nets, mate? The fish, during their spawning season, let them spawn so they can multiply, but no, they want to wipe them out, mate... I always used to say: "Look, son, education is the future, fishing is not the future." Fishing is a way of life, not a livelihood.

So, he dedicated himself to studying. And another thing: "What I went through, I don't want you to go through, son." Because it's tough, mate... going through a storm at night without being able to sleep. Because what they're doing is cruel. It's suffering, mate... Fishing in small canoes...

He paused to wet his whistle with another swig and continued his sermon of wisdom:

- We only sell from four in the afternoon, because the sun is cooler. We bring the fish from the lake; we don't really refrigerate it. We take a bit of ice because, in this summer heat, tucunaré gets spoiled. Sometimes we don't even sell the fish, mate... we do four, five rounds, sometimes we sell one, two. I come back the next day to fish again. I tell my wife to share with her sisters, or I send it to my brothers in Itaúna. That's how it's better, so the fish doesn't spoil.

- Seu Joacir is right - commented Coreolano, also a riverside fisherman, addressing the elderly speaker: - You speak for all of us. You can stand up for us at City Hall and complain about the floods. The waters are getting to our homes, mate... Where's the Mayor? He should come and see.

The assembly approved the idea by raising their arms, waving bottles of cachaça. Almost all the houses in the neighbourhood were built on stilts, but this year the floods arrived earlier and are already a few centimetres from invading them. How many times, before every election, had they been promised the construction of dykes to contain the Amazon's waters?

Since before the arrival of the colonisers, the riverside peoples had engaged in subsistence fishing, catching only according to their daily needs. There was never a shortage of fish in the Amazon, with a wide variety of species in the flooded igapó forests and the igarapés, where the water stretches as far as the eye can see from February to July, during the flood season.

In January, the waters start to recede, retreating to the riverbed, leaving behind "coios," fishing lakes that the fishermen share with the caimans trapped there.

Coreolano had started fishing with his father when he was 8 years old, as was tradition, the craft being passed from father to son. He had never attended school. His father's rowing canoe was his school, and his father was the teacher in the school of life.

Over time, he perfected the art of rod fishing, assembling longlines with hooks, making spears with harpoons, weaving the "passaguá" nets, and mending gillnets.

He learned to recognise perhaps a hundred types of fish from the Amazon, but the ones he most frequently catches, consumes, and sells, are pirarucu, piranha, arapaima, aruanã, payara, tucunaré, and surubim. As he became an adult and began selling surplus fish, he saved up enough money to buy a second-hand "rabeta" (longtail boat) with a petrol engine, which allows him to go further in search of fish and prepare to send his children, Luana and Odacir, to study in the big city, either in Manaus or Belém, in any case without leaving behind the river that is their home.

1999

Parintins. Amazon River

When Luana was not yet attending school, her brother spent all day with her, playing in the street with other girls of their age. Odacir preferred being with them rather than playing with the other boys, who enjoyed typical boys' games, like football with a makeshift ball and two stones marking the goals. Everyone wanted to be like Ronaldinho Gaúcho or Maradona. They alternated with playing with toy cars, marble games, and wrestling matches, games of strength and agility that revealed some aggression, even at a young age.

Little Odacir preferred the girls' games, like peteca (a traditional Brazilian shuttlecock game), skipping rope, ciranda-cirandinha (a circle dance), and hopscotch. His mother found it odd but felt more at ease knowing he was always under his sister's watch and not at risk from the more dangerous games, which sometimes ended in minor injuries.

Coreolano, who was absent most of the day due to fishing and then selling the catch, never noticed his son's choice of games, and the mother, fearing her husband's rough reaction, never mentioned it to him.

When Luana, two years older than Odacir, started primary school, the mother took the opportunity to help her husband and brought the boy along so he could get used to fishing.

Although Coreolano had plans to educate his children if they wished and had the aptitude, he believed it wouldn't hurt the boy to learn the riverside fishing craft, an essential skill for survival.

Young Odacir enjoyed accompanying his parents to the river. Early in the morning, he happily jumped into the "rabeta" (a small boat) and carefully observed all his father's manoeuvres as they travelled up and down the river until he decided on a spot to cast the net.

Odacir wanted to stay busy and, from the first day, insisted on trying his luck with a fishing rod. He would beam with joy when a piranha or a small jaraqui wriggled at the end of the line. But one day, he had a huge scare that almost sent him overboard when he hooked a payara, though small, with its open mouth and sharp long teeth, terrifying him. His father had a good laugh at his fright.

Odacir was a cheerful child until he started school at seven. In his first year, he began to feel something different about himself compared to the other boys. He had noticed it before but couldn't explain why, which saddened him. During breaks, he interacted little with the other boys. He always refused to play football, to jump over the swing, or join in the races and shoving matches, which started drawing the attention of his classmates. After a few months, he heard the word "sissy" directed at him for the first time. The insult left him deeply shocked and reluctant to return to school. He began to hide during breaks rather than face the boys' taunts.

Iracema, one occasion, had found her son playing with his sister's dolls. She scolded him and forbade him from touching them again. Embarrassed but eager to please his mother, he promised not to play with them anymore.

The most troubling moment came when his mother caught him wearing his sister's clothes. That's when he gathered the courage and, with a timid voice, almost inaudible, but with the honesty and innocence of a child, said:

- Mum, I am a girl.

Iracema chose not to alert her husband to the issue with their son. She feared his impulsive reaction, unsure of what he might do. The intolerance and rejection of such rare cases, whispered about in hushed tones, were well known. No one was prepared to face the neighbors reactions.

The first person Iracema thought of to "cure" her son of this terrible affliction was old Doctor Gusmão, who should have long been retired but still held consultations daily. He was a revered healer in the community, especially by the fishing community, and he didn't charge the needy for consultations.

Without ever saying anything to her husband, she took advantage of the morning hours when he was out fishing and took her son to see the Doctor. Embarrassed, she explained the situation.

- This is a tough case, said the Doctor. Let me speak to the boy alone. Wait outside.

Attentive and understanding of the severity of the problem, the old doctor asked the boy to explain his problems.

- I'm ashamed of my willy. It's such an ugly thing. Do you think it will fall off with age?

- Let's have a look. No, nothing like that. Your willy is perfectly normal.

- I don't know, but I don't like it, nor the balls. They're useless because I think I'm a girl.

- Do you pee standing up or sitting down?

- I prefer sitting.

- And you like to wear girls' clothes, don't you?

- I do.

The old Doctor ran his hands over his white-crowned head. He had heard enough.

- Dona Iracema, you may come in; I want to speak with you.

Iracema entered, visibly shaken and unable to hide her anxiety.

- What do you think, Doctor?

- The boy suffers from a mental disorder known as Gender Identity Disorder. He was born a boy but wants to be a girl.

- And that can't be cured, Doctor?

- There are treatments, but that is the responsibility of specialists. Only a psychiatrist can help him, but there isn't one here in Parintins. You will have to take him to Manaus or Belém.

- And are many treatments needed? It's so far away!

- It could take years and might not even work. For some, the condition is incurable, no matter how many treatments they undergo. It's possible that when he becomes an adult, he will still want to be a woman, and there's nothing that can be done about it.

If she only needed to go to Manaus once or twice, she could always justify it to her husband by saying she was visiting her sick sister, but more frequent trips would be hard to explain. Knowing that it might not work plunged Iracema into deep disappointment, but she was determined to do everything she could to help her son.

Iracema, honouring her Indigenous ancestral origins, despite being raised as a Catholic, believes in the ancient knowledge of the Indigenous people of the Amazon to cure certain ailments that doctors can not.

The caboclo shamans derive from Indigenous shamans, heirs to the knowledge and traditions of the Tupinambá. They are considered special men, capable of communicating with the dead, spirits, and ancestors, from whom they receive knowledge to heal all kinds of unknown ailments, spells, pains, love issues, jealousy, or bad luck, in rituals involving massages, puffs of tobacco smoke over the patient's body, dances, and singing. She sought out the prayer ground of the healer Torcato, a famous shaman in the region, to whom she explained, with a fervent request for confidentiality, the situation of the boy.

With the session scheduled for the next day, the healer appeared dressed in Indigenous ornaments, with amulets and bone necklaces, and his head crowned with macaw feathers. He began to dance and shake a maraca, making sounds to call upon the beyond, in an evident altered state of consciousness, for which he had previously taken a potion made from sacred jurema acacia and psychedelic mushrooms, intended to enter a shamanic trance to communicate with the dead.

To restore the patient's balance, he placed human faeces on his navel, then massaged it all over the boy's naked body, laid out on a mat on the ground, expelling the evil. The boy endured the treatment patiently.

To finish, the shaman shook a staff pointed at the sky, with an amuncuré fruit at the tip, to summon the spirits. A long silence followed, respectfully awaiting the spirits to act.

Two weeks later, Iracema, already impatient, inquired for the tenth time about the treatment's results.

- So, son. Don't you want to be a girl anymore? Don't you feel cured?

- No, mother, I haven't been cured. Everything is the same.

In Iracema's mind, there was no doubt that her son's illness could only be the result of witchcraft, of black umbanda, or voodoo that envious neighbors, had done to the boy, jealous of the money her husband makes selling fish. Money that, in reality, barely covers the household expenses.

Just in case, since it wouldn't do him harm, she decided to go to the tent of sinhazinha Aparecida to seek advice on the most suitable remedy for her son, who suffers from a mental illness that is not clearly defined.

Sinhazinha has on display more than a hundred little bottles hanging from the ceiling, which were once used for perfumes or cachaça and now contain liquids of various colors with labels indicating the treatments they are for, charms for all kinds of love, luck and spells.

Among the vast variety of offerings, Iracema went through reading all the labels, some handwritten by Sinhazinha herself, who creates them with the knowledge that makes her a recognized healer:

Come to me

Hold wealthy husband

Call wealthy husband

Raise stick

I will succeed

Call money

Catch man

Catch woman

Lucky talisman

Breack

Love elixir

Break spell

- That's exactly what the boy needs. Give me a bottle of Break Spell and another of Break Envy.

The charms didn't work, but Iracema didn't give up.

She knows that although macumba is of African origin, it's not only black people who believe in it. In Brazil, and particularly in the Amazon, the Amerindians converted to Catholicism blend, with total naturalness, into a religious syncretism, African traditions with the saints and doctrines of the Church and spiritism. In umbanda, a Brazilian derivation of macumba, the fetishist ceremony of African origin with Christian influence is dedicated to the worship of Orixás, deities that, in popular belief, are one and the same as the saints of the Church:

Oxalá, who is the syncretism of Jesus

Iemanjá, Our Lady of Navigators and Fishermen

Xangô, Saint John the Baptist

Oxúm, Our Lady of Aparecida

Ogúm, Saint George

Oxóssi, Saint Sebastien

Ibeji, Saint Cosmas

Omulu/Obaluanyê, Saint Lazarus

Iansã, Saint Barbara

Nanã, Daint Anne

Oxumaré, Saint Bartolomew

Exu, Saint Antony.

Iracema asked when the next session would be at Mãe Bena's terreiro. Her native title is Yalorixá, or Mother of Saints. She is a medium capable of communicating between humans and spirits during the religious rituals she performs three times a week at her terreiro, which is attached to her own residence.

Just as masses can be ordered and paid for in the Catholic Church, believers can also ask the Mother of Saints for the ceremony to be dedicated to the Orixá of their devotion, requesting that they intercede on behalf of someone, usually to heal a serious illness, as Iracema had requested for little Odacir.

The umbanda ceremony to which she took her son to pray to Oxalá (Jesus) naturally had to be paid for because the work of the Mother of Saints must be compensated, in addition to the involvement of several participants, all dressed in white, like the initiated, Children of Saints, and the three Ogãs, the musicians playing the atabaques. The attending public, who also pays, includes some curious tourists as well as believers.

During the ceremony, the Mother of Saints and the public danced, sang, drank cachaça, and smoked cigarettes under the influence of the spirits, to the sound of the atabaques, which initially set a moderate rhythm but evolved into a crescendo until it became frantic, to the point of inducing the Mother of Saints and some of the initiated into a trance.

In an attempt to bring little Odacir, already exhausted from the frenetic dancing, into a trance to communicate with Oxalá, a Child of Saints followed him all the time, shaking a xequeré over his head, making the dried seeds inside the gourd rattle, until he made him dizzy and fall to the ground, which the Mother of Saints ultimately considered a successful communication with Oxalá.

- So, son. Do you think you are cured?

- I think nothing has changed, mother.

- Do you still believe you are a girl?

- This has all been a great confusion for me, but I think I do.

In despair, Iracema went to confess at the church farthest from her home, where the priest did not know her. She knew that whatever she told him in confession, he couldn't tell anyone.

In the privacy of the confessional, she explained what she was there for. When he realized she didn't want to confess but rather seek advice, he told her to step out of the confessional and they would speak outside.

She refused, always hiding her face at an angle where the priest wouldn't recognize her.

Understanding the reason for her shame, he decided to respect her privacy and continue the conversation inside the confessional, never looking at her.

- I've tried everything. Even Jesus failed me when I asked for help in the form of Oxalá.

- It might be more correct to think that it wasn't Jesus who failed you, but the intermediary. Instead of going to the source, asking Jesus, at church or at home, you went to a pagan source that has nothing to do with Jesus. These are popular superstitions.

- But I am nobody to speak to Him. That's why I went to the Mother of Saints. Couldn't you, Father, make the request for me? You speak to Him, don't you?

- Look, since the doctors can't solve the issue for you, what you need to do is pray a lot and surround your son with good people who set an example of life and guide him towards Jesus, who heals all. I think the best thing would be to send the boy to a religious school. He could even continue his studies at the seminary. Even if he later doesn't want to be a priest, he will discover the path of righteousness and virtue, far from bad influences and the temptations of the devil. With good examples and discipline, he will be able to achieve spiritual healing from the sin that has entered him.

2000

Belém do Pará

Iracema had a hard time explaining to her husband why they should send their young son to study far away. It had been part of Coreolano's plan to send his son to secondary school or technical school, if he wanted to learn a trade, in Manaus or Belém, but only when he was 15, after completing the nine mandatory years of primary education in Parintins.

Anticipating her husband's reaction, Iracema had prepared little Odacir to explain to his father that he would like a religious education and might even want to become a priest in the future.

- See? The boy has a calling, and if he becomes a priest, he'll have a guaranteed future. He won't have to live a poor life. Have you ever seen a priest in need?

The following school year, at the age of 8, little Odacir entered the Virgin Aparecida boarding school, in Belém do Pará, run by the religious order The Legionaries of Christ, which had been founded in Mexico but already existed in several countries where it ran numerous schools and some seminaries.

From then on, he would rarely see his parents, only during school holidays, as he would have to travel by boat for three and a half days upriver on the Amazon. His father would need to sell a lot of fish to pay for the journeys.

Once settled into school, he promised himself he would do everything to fit into the identity that his mother, his new teachers, and, ultimately, the whole of society expected of him, to be a boy in training to become a true man, the pride of the family.

At the time, he believed the world must be right and that he must be the one who was wrong for wanting to be a girl. Under the influence of his surroundings, he accepted that he suffered from a strange mental illness, and to cure himself, he decided to comply with all the behavior rules that school and natural interaction with his peers demanded.

He began wanting to play football, but he was rarely chosen for the pick-up teams, due to his lack of skill, as recognized by his classmates. Worried that this might lead to teasing or marginalization, he informed his Physical Education teacher that he preferred to focus on gymnastics and athletics instead of team sports.

In this way, he could avoid the group competition that gave rise to some aggression, considered a normal expression of masculinity and virility. In gymnastics and athletics, he would only have to compete with himself and wouldn't have to face aggressive situations.

He went on to excel in gymnastics for his skill and speed at rope climbing and vaulting; in athletics, he stood out for his ease in high jumping and was the school champion, in his age group, in the 100 meter sprint and 100 meter hurdles. Only two students were better than him, one aged 17 and the other 18.

His public affirmation of masculinity was thus secured, which he interpreted as the path to a possible cure for an illness that, in reality, he had never truly felt.

It resulted in a disturbing, ongoing identity conflict, the recognition of his male physique, which continued to displease him and contradicted a deep, inner feeling that, despite his efforts to adapt to the requirements of his birth gender, kept insinuating itself into his consciousness as feminine.

Such a conflict forced him into a clandestine inner life that prevented him from revealing his own identity to the world, which made him permanently sad, introspective, reserved, and self-isolated from cheerful interactions with his peers.

The teachers did not attribute importance to this noticeable fact, as he proved to be a good student and succeeded in gymnastics and athletics. They thought it was likely a natural difficulty for a child of Amerindian origin, raised in the Amazon jungle, to adapt to the environment, practices, and customs of a big city.

During his first year at school, Odacir noticed, though he paid it no mind, that every so often, the head priest would come at night to the dormitory where 30 boys aged 8 to 10 slept and call one of them to go to his office.

- It must be to tell them off for getting bad marks or for doing something wrong, Odacir thought, falling asleep unconcerned, confident in his good grades and his trouble-free behavior. In the morning, when they woke up, everyone was in their beds, and the subject was never discussed.

In another dormitory, were the students aged 11 to 15, and in yet another, those aged 16 to 18. They had breaks at different times, and there was little contact between students of different age groups. In the dining hall, they all ate at the same time, as did the teachers, but in areas separated by age groups.

It seemed to Odacir that the school wanted to avoid contact between students of different ages. He didn't quite understand why, but the priests must know best.

1941-2002

The Legionaires of Christ

The Legionaries of Christ religious congregation, also known as the Legion of Christ, was founded in 1941 in Mexico City by Father Marcial Maciel Degollado and was approved by the Holy See in 1965 by Pope Paul VI.

Over time, the congregation expanded to several countries. In 1980, it already owned 214 religious schools dedicated to the formation of official education, and had 17 seminars run by priests who had been trained by Father Marcial.

Since the beginning of his ministry, the founder of the congregation indulged in sexual practices with adult women and minors, school students. It was discovered that he sexually abused 60 boys between the ages of 11 and 16, including his own children, which he had from two women.

A letter from a former priest of the Legion of Christ was sent to the Vatican denouncing Martial's pedophile abuse but there was never a response and nothing happened.

In addition to the founder, the names of 33 legionary priests and 71 seminarians who sexually abused 175 minors over decades became known, in a process of chain rapes, in which the victims of abuse later became perpetrators. There are first, second and third generation victims.

One of the most poignant reports of abuse by legionary priests was made by Ana Lúcia Salazar, Mexican television presenter and mother of three children, about the abuse that occurred at the Instituto Cumbres, in the city of Cancun, by Father Fernando Martinez Suaréz on girls among six and nine years old, in the 90s. She reported that when she was eight years old, she saw the school administrator go to the classrooms and call girls to go to the chapel to confess to Father Martinez.

"While some were reading the Bible, he raped the others in front of them, little girls of six, eight or nine years old." - she said.

The priest was removed to Rome, where he managed to escape civil and ecclesiastical courts.

Only later, did the Vatican recognize the crimes committed by Father Marcial. Considering his advanced age, Pope Benedict XVI ordered him to retire to a life of "prayer and penance" in a luxurious mansion in Jacksonville, Florida.

Despite this, Benedict XVI did not respond to requests to dissolve the Legion of Christ.

At a session of the UN Committee for the Rights of the Child, the Vatican was asked to suspend the canonization of John Paul II, given his inaction and cover-up of the Church's many other sexual abuses.

2002

Belém do Pará

The novice Délcio Cavalcanti, at 18 years old, was finishing the 12th year of his secondary education, at the Virgem Aparecida school. In addition to the official teaching subjects, he had undergone extensive preparatory training for the following year, to enter the Seminary of the Legionaries of Christ, in Curitiba.

He had come to the conclusion that his future would be the priesthood, in the service of his religious institution and a career in teaching at one of their several schools spread across Brazil.

There was more calculation in him than vocation, as he wanted to guarantee a safe and secure job, in a noble and respectable career, far from the poverty of his family origins, without worries about financial survival, security for life and absolute impunity to continue his addictive practice inherited from the fact that he was raped by the school principal, when he was 10 years old, that he continued to be one of his favorites and won special privileges awarded to those who pleased the superior.

Eight years of continued sexual practice with the director, who confessed he had been raped by the institution's founder, Father Marcial, made it clear that what had begun as a violent surprise and discovery for himself, became an affirmation of mutual pleasure from the awakening of puberty.

He ended up accepting the situation normally, realizing that it was a natural expression of sexuality for priests who cannot marry. He himself, from the age of fifteen, started raping little boys at school, around 9, 10 years old. Everything happened with description and there had never been any complaints from any of the boys who, embarrassed, feared being expelled and having to explain to their parents the experience they had been through.

At the beginning of the second year of school, Odacir, then 9 years old, had not yet awakened to puberty, which would only start for himself about a year later. Although he continued to feel like a girl in the wrong body of a boy, this had, for now, no affirmation of sexual orientation, it was more a generic question of affirmation of identity. Therefore, he was unaware of the sexual tension that had not yet awakened, in addition to a vague and ill-defined curiosity about the differences between the sexes, which is natural for someone who is developing their personality in relation to the world around himself

Secretly, he continued to feel like a girl although, consciously and at the mercy of social pressure, he accepted that perhaps he suffered from a mental illness, as that was what everyone thought about the matter.

The most believing and religious, like the priests at the school, thought about this issue, without knowing the problem, that it was a sin against nature that needed to be corrected.

Whether it was a mental illness or not, the truth is that it seemed to him that he would live his whole life with it, but the fact of having to hide the identity that he felt was his, caused him a permanent state of anxiety, insecurity, sadness and isolation.

On weekends, school students who did not go home were allowed to go outside for a few hours, with younger students being advised not to stray too far from the area.

In those days there were always fewer people at school. In addition to those who went home, others were visited by family who took them to a walk and spend the day outside.

Odacir never went home, except on long holidays, due to the distance and the price of boat tickets. He did his best to entertain himself, reading in the library, or watching TV Globo programs and competitions in the living room, or playing table tennis with other student who was also at school. Other times he would run to improve is times on the track.

After one of these solitary training sessions, he went to the locker room to take a shower and change his clothes.

In the middle of the bath, although without seeing anyone, he instinctively senses that he is being watched.

2002

Belém do Pará

Odacir was right when he felt he was being watched in the shower. His first reaction was to turn off the tap and cover himself with a towel around his waist.

Surprised, he saw an older student approach him, whom he only knew by sight, in the cafeteria. Assuming he was coming to take a shower, he hurried to dry his body with a towel, although he wondered why the other boy didn't go to one of the several cabins, all of which were empty.

The older boy ostensibly stood to block the exit door of the cabin where Odacir was, and spoke:

- What is your name?

- Odacir

- You still don't paint. Are you already horny?

- What?

- Have you touched the animal, yet?

Upset, Odacir did not respond.

- Have you already cut the peach tree?

Without responding, little Odacir hurried to get dressed to get out of there as quickly as possible.

The older boy grabbed his arm, stopping him from getting dressed.

- Let yourself be like this, you're fine.

- What do you want?

- I'm the one asking the questions. Have you already been baptized?

Finding the question strange, which didn't come to anything, he simply replied, timidly:

- Yes.

- Who baptized you?

- I don't know. How could I remember? I was still a baby.

- That's not the baptism I'm referring to. Here at school, hasn't anyone baptized you yet?

- Why should I be baptized again?

- You're a little angel. I already saw that you are a virgin waiting to be debuted. I'm the one who's going to baptize you, I like to blow the shit out of boys like you.

Odacir woke up in a room that served as the school's infirmary. He had been found passed out on the floor of one of the shower cabins, by an employee who was cleaning and went to call the director.

A doctor that was watching him used to be called to the school when someone was hurt or sick.

His whole body and head hurt, but worse than that, his soul hurt. Added to the state of physical prostration was an indescribable discomfort, fear, insecurity, a need to escape, which was expressed in a single statement:

- I want to go home. I want my parents.

The doctor informed the director of what was clearly visible in the boy. A series of bruises all over his body, a bruise on his head and a bleeding anus left no doubt as to what had happened.

- Dear doctor Ciro. Not a word out there about what happened, if you want to keep working for us. This is not a matter for the police. We solve the internal problems.

- And you, my boy, have no business going home. You won't worry your parents. And don't tell anyone about it. Do you realize they're going to think you're a sissy? Aren't you ashamed of people calling you a sissy? We will take care of you and punish the culprit. Who was the guy?

- I don't know what it's called. All I know is that he's one of the older ones, who is usually seen in the cafeteria.

- So, you stay here in recovery for a day or two and then go identify him in the cafeteria. He will be punished, you will see.

Finalist Délcio Cavalcanti, a long-time faithful servant of the director's lustful needs, before whom he was on his knees, not to pray with him but to satisfy an urgency, stood up and apologized:

- Godfather, I know I overdid myself a bit, but it happened. I promise it won't happen again.

- I can't let this slip of yours go unnoticed. It would be very noticeable if you didn't suffer any punishment.

- But, godfather, what about my going to the Seminary?

- Don't worry, let's do it like this: as there are only two months left for you to finish the course, you will be expelled from school, so I can set an example. You go to your parents' house but don't worry because you have more than enough grades to pass the year and finish the course. In October, you enter the Seminar but you have to promise me that you will start doing things with the utmost discretion.

The punishment of Délcio's expulsion did nothing to minimize the trauma that the incident had caused to young Odacir.

After asking other colleagues if they knew of more cases like his, and learning that it was a common practice, both on the part of older students, teachers and the director himself, although without resorting to violence, his state of spirit began to oscillate between shock, nausea, anger and a deep depression, which he experienced when he concluded that he had to react like an adult if he wanted to survive the jungle that surrounded him.

He promised himself that he would be able to defend himself the next time he might be harassed.

Going home, having to explain why, was something that would not be possible. He didn't even want to give his parents this displeasure, nor would he know how to face them with shame, even though it wasn't his fault. Although he was still a fragile boy, compared to the physiognomy of older students and adults, he would have to find a way to defend himself from possible new attacks.

He would have to arm himself…but how?

In a practical crafts class at the Virgem Aparecida school, he found a Xato with a retractable blade. Perfect.

2002

Belém do Pará

Odacir finished the school year at Virgem Aparecida school. He received the money his father sent to buy the boat trip to Parintins, to go on vacation with the family.

It's Sunday and the young boy decided to take a walk to the port to buy the ticket for the next day trip. He wants to avoid the crowds at departure time, the usual confusion of everyone boarding, loaded with bags with the most diverse goods to take home.

There are a huge number of modest wooden boats, moored, that provide public transport up the river, making stops to drop off and receive passengers and cargo throughout the many small towns along the Amazon River. The boats do not have cabins for passengers. They accommodate themselves in the outdoor space and spend the night sleeping in suspended hammocks, next to their personal cargo, which cannot be lost of sight.

After buying the ticket, Odacir took the opportunity to move away from the boarding area, always popular with tourists, to enter the fishing boat area, which on a Sunday afternoon, floated along with the gentle swell, moored on a resting day for most of the fishermen.

In that deserted area on Sunday, he liked to wander around the boats, distract himself observing each one of them and remember with pleasure the times he spent fishing with his parents.

He was between two boats that were being dried for repairs when he was surprised by a voice behind him:

- Oh! My son of a bitch! You'll pay for it. I was expelled from school because of you.

Délcio advanced towards Odacir with a threatening air. The little one even thought about running away but found himself trapped between the two boats, with no space to get out on the other side. He realized that he would have to face the situation, he took a deep breath and concentrated on what he had to do.

He decided to remain quiet, in the same place, waiting for the other boy's reaction. In a natural movement, without showing agitation, he put his right hand in the back pocket of his shorts and waited.

- You're going to take a beating and I'm going to leave you dead, but first, you're going to give me a blow job. Get on your knees, big bitch. He approached the little one, at the same time as he unbuttoned and lowered his pants.

- Come on, suck it, son of a bitch.

Odacir obeyed, kneeling before him.

When the assailant brought his sex closer to his mouth, in the blink of an eye, Odacir delivered a long blow with the Xacto, which missed the target.

The intention, which he had dreamed of since he was raped, was to cut the base of the instrument that had tortured him and leave the assailant sexually disabled for the rest of his life, prevented from raping any more defenseless children.

But Délcio, belatedly realizing the blow, still tried to escape to the side and the blade made a cut of more than ten centimeters in his groin, which made him let out a scream of pain.

Odacir took the opportunity to run away, only realizing that the other had fallen to the ground holding his groin which was gushing profusely. He ran, ran, ran, and only stopped, exhausted, upon arrival at school, in a state of uncontrollable nervousness. He took refuge in bed, hidden under the sheet, while he cried and trembled compulsively, asking God for forgiveness for the sin he had committed but would never confess to anyone.

The next day, Odacir left for his parents who were waiting for him with great longing. He calmed down during the trip, trusting that the damned Décio was fine, that he had been helped and taken to a hospital.

It didn't occur to him that the blow to the groin could have deadly consequences, nor did he want to have on his conscience the death of anyone, even the despicable Délcio. Once at home, with his family, he decided not to worry anymore, thinking about the case. It hapened, he would try to forget it.

And that no other sexual predator would make him use Xacto again. What he didn't know was that a deep blow cutting the femoral artery, in just a few minutes, causes a blood loss that leads to death in a very short time.

On Monday, early in the morning, still dark at night, when the first fishermen from Belém went to their boats to start their fishing work, they found an inanimate boy, curled up on himself, immersed in a pool of blood.

They called an ambulance with a doctor who declared death at the scene and a police van, took care of the incident. Nothing unusual in Brazil. There are so many minors murdered during the year that they do not always give rise to police investigations.

The policemen limit themselves to trying to identify the boy to notify the parents and hand over the body to them. Unless they are the children of someone important, each murder of minors, in most cases, does not even trigger an investigation.

Only in the case of rape of minors, followed by murder, the Penal Code provides for heavy penalties, which can reach up to 30 years in prison, if the victims are under 14 years of age.

2005

Rio de Janeiro

Dorival Avelar De Angelis mourned his beloved mother on the day of her funeral. The coffin was accompanied to its last resting place by a small crowd of anonymous admirers, high-ranking figures from industry and banking, artists, and all the big names in Rio de Janeiro's high society, as well as some of the wealthiest families from around the world.

From France, condolences arrived from the houses Pierre Cardim, Givenchy, Yves Saint Laurent, Azzaro and Valentino, who did not forget Maitê's collaboration, initially as a mannequin who lived in Paris for 20 years, then became a regular customer and more faithful in his fashion shows and establishing personal friendships with the greatest designers of haute couture.

After the funeral service ended, in the confines of his home, Dorival could not help but remember the privileged life of his mother, Maitê Avelar De Angelis, born from wealthy families. She was a descendant of the Brazilian rural aristocracy of the 19th century, from the Baron of Goiana, on his father's side, and the Duchess of Ceará, on his mother's side, noble titles passed from parents to children, as well as their vast estates, in a country where only 1% of rural landowners own 45% of the entire rural area.

She was not yet 30 years old when Maitê had already inherited 18 agricultural farms, some with more than 10 thousand hectares, 2 sugar mills and a gold mine. The problem was that she had no knowledge, nor the vocation to learn how to manage rural properties or mining. Handed over to foremen who were already part of the farms, they quickly degenerated into an uncontrolled robbery, starting to show debts instead of income. It was her husband, Tony Brancaamp De Angelis, who put an end to the situation, ending up selling all the properties, for valuable money that reinforced

Maitê's existing fortune. With the business of supplying weapons to the army, since the Paraguayan War, from 1864 to 1870, his father, Antenor De Angelis, had accumulated a considerable fortune that provided Tony with a bohemian life of sumptuous spending, being an organizer of hunts in Africa to which he invited friends, bearing all expenses. Once married to Maitê, they spent most of their time at their home in Paris, where they organized sumptuous parties, with the cream of the aristocracy and European high society as guests. They even rented palaces to hold their parties, not only in France, but also in England, Austria and even castles in Africa. Participating in their parties were Princess Diana and Prince Charles, King Constantine of Greece, Princess Soraya of Iran, members of the richest families in the world, such as the Rothschilds, the Onassis and the Roquefellers, fashion designers such as Yves Saint Laurent, writers like Truman Capote, Hollywood artists like Clark Gable. They rented the supersonic Concorde to transport their guests to gala dinners or hunting trips in Africa.

Maitê Avelar De Angelis, who dressed exclusively in haute couture, was considered the reference of good taste and elegance, while the wasteful extravagance of the charming playboy Tony also attracted the pink press. The most famous fashion magazine, American Vogue, considered the couple Maitê and Tony as the most chic couple in the world. The old Antenor died and his son, never used to working, saw his control over the arms business progressively being lost, to the point of losing the representations he had and the income tap being closed, at the same time that the sumptuous expenses were not decreased. Not wanting to worry his wife and not accepting to reduce, in any way, his quality of life, Tony hid the closure of the weapons business from Maitê and then decided to resort to his wife's fortune to continue enjoying the same type of life.

It was only then that Maitê's banker friend announced that her fortune was being squandered that she became aware of the real financial situation. Fortunately, still in time to save a large nest egg for her future and for her son Dorival.

Maitê demanded a divorce, leaving the house in Paris to her husband and keeping the thousand square meter apartment in Rio de Janeiro, on Avenida Atlantida, front of Copacabana beach, with 24-hour armed security and entrance by private elevator. She put an end to the big parties but, in return, she became the guest at all the parties and gala dinners organized by Brazilian high society. Her international fame as a great lady made it mandatory to be invited to any party that wanted to be covered in the press. Above all, after publishing the "Savoir Faire" etiquette manual, there would be no worthy parties without his presence. She was the reference of good tone and chic that all of high society wanted to imitate. If she did not accept an invitation, it was certain and known that the party would go unnoticed in the press.

If she was present, the presence of paparazzi and journalists was guaranteed.

She was usually accompanied by her only son, Dorival, whom she had adopted as a baby, because she did not want to distort her body with pregnancy.

Dorival, then became known to all of high society and was pampered as the son of a great lady, accepting naturally and without the slightest criticism his known homosexuality.

What in the lower classes was ridiculed, despised and the target of persecution, violence and even torture, in the upper classes was even considered a sign of high artistic sensitivity and refinement.

2005 to 210

Parintins

Returning to Parintins, Odacir resumed his studies and wanting to earn some money, from the age of 15, he convinced his father to lend him the boat to take tourists fishing piranhas in the streams, which he advertised in handwritten leaflets, pasted on the walls of the neighbors buildings of the city, in main hotels and close to the port, where they disembarked. He quickly became known and started taking trips on the weekends, when his father didn't need the boat. He began to earn some money and meet people from outside, mostly foreigners, from whom he tried to learn something about their countries.

Faced with the ultra-conservative mentality of inland locations, economically and socially disadvantaged, and alien to modernism and the dissolution of ancestral values, habits and customs, typical of large cities and wealthier social classes, Parintins, a small city, but already with 116,000 people inhabitants, remained as if stagnant in time, with regard to intolerance against the slightest alteration to the natural order of divine creation, in which a man is a man and a woman is a woman, with no third sex existing which, to
manifest if so, it would have to be repudiated as unnatural.

Odacir understood perfectly that it would never be in his homeland that he would feel free to express his sexual orientation and that he would have to protect his personal safety while living there.

He promised himself that, while he lived with his parents in Parintins, he would do everything he could to hide his gender identity.
On the other hand, always fearing that he would be discovered and fearing the consequences, he decided that it was time to stop carrying a box cutter in his pocket, although it was normal for a boy his age to carry a pocket knife,

more like a utility knife for multiple uses, typical of the male condition, than as a bladed weapon.

He thought that what he needed was to gain self-confidence and acquire self-defense skills in case of potential future attacks, which only the practice of a martial art would allow him to do.

He initially thought about learning capoeira but, as it was practiced, in the tradition of the slaves who created it, based on African culture, although it was intended to fight the thugs of slave bosses, it only had the appearance of a ritual and folkloric dance, in order to be authorized by white people who had no idea that it was a martial art, capable of taking down an enemy, even if he was mounted on a horse.

Traditional capoeira, still practiced today, does not complete the strikes by impacting the opponent, limiting itself to performing them without ever reaching the target. It continues to seem just like a dance, when, at the current moment, nothing more justifies its reality as a martial art being hidden. It continues to exist, mostly for display to tourists and to extort money from those who want to photograph the spectacle.

Therefore, it would not be capoeira that would give him the self-defense capacity he wanted.

He discovered that a martial arts center had opened in Parintins where an instructor taught Uru-Can. He tried to find out what it was about. It is a mixed martial art, created within the Brazilian army with elements of Karate, Taekwondo, Kung Fu, Judo and Jiu-Jitsu, for self-defense against attacks with sticks, knives and firearms.

When Odacir informed his parents that he had enrolled in a martial arts school, his mother's surprise and his father's pride were great, as he saw his son's status as a macho man confirmed.

Whether due to social pressure, or due to the change in age that he had suffered in the last years of his still short life, once he had awakened his sexuality, he began to notice, with surprise, that, in addition to continuing to feel that he was a girl in a male body, he was equally awakened by lustful desires, whether for boys or for girls.

He began sexual activity when he was 15 years old, with a girl from the city, he liked it and then he had occasional relationships with another, and with another, and with another, which earned him the reputation of a womanizer, in his circle of relationships, which reached in the father's ears, increasingly proud of his son's virility.

From the age of 16, always in great secrecy, he had occasional and fleeting relationships with boys and adult men, all of them foreign tourists whom he had met as a guide on boat trips, which confirmed that they gave him the same pleasure as the girls.

He swore to himself that, with people of the same sex, he would only have relationships with tourists, covering up the purpose of his presence in the hotels with supposed meetings with clients to organize the fishing trip. He would never have a relationship there with anyone from Parintins, not even Brazilian.

Seeking to discover himself in his gender identification, after countless searches on the Internet, reading articles on the subject, he learned that, according to the ICD - International Statistical Classification of Diseases and Related Health Problems, released by Wikiwand, regarding gender identity disorders in children, "Only a small number of diagnosed children continue to have gender identity disorder into adolescence and adulthood". With the influence of school, family and community, the behaviors of the opposite sex are generally repressed and boys become more masculine and girls more feminine.

- Odacir recognized that this was what was happening to him. About 75% of boys have a homosexual or bisexual sexual orientation in adulthood and about 25% remains heterosexual.

- That's right - thought Odacir, given the fact that he felt attracted, whether to boys or girls.

Those who become transvestites or transgenders, usually start later, in adolescence or adulthood.

2011

Rio de Janeiro

After completing his compulsory education studies, Odacir informed his parents that he intended to take the tourist guide course, which, as it did not exist in Parintins, forced him to go to a big city.

Over the three years he took tourists fishing for piranhas, he saved a sum of money that would allow him to live in Rio de Janeiro for a while, even if he wouldn't find a job soon. His idea was to work during the day and attend the course at night.

As soon as he arrived in Rio, his first concern was finding a place to live, the price of which within his reach.

Consulting the advertisements in the newspapers, he found that even in a favela, what he could hardly afford, would be a 30 square meter kitchenette apartment but completely empty of furniture and kitchen equipment, which was beyond his means to buy. Equipped and furnished spaces reached absolutely prohibitive prices.

He found a column of ads from people looking for other people to share an apartment with.

He called several of them to find out prices and conditions, until he decided to go and see a house in the Rocinha favela, in the South Zone, where live 70 thousand inhabitants.

When looking for the address, he quickly realized that it was an area with the greatest poverty and population density. The streets are so narrow that they barely let in sunlight, there is a lack of basic sanitation, and tuberculosis proliferates.

He didn't like the look of the neighborhood, it wasn't a place he wanted to live but, as long as he didn't have a job, he had no choice but to accept the only price he could pay.

He found a one-story house, with exposed brick walls, which had never been plastered or painted, with iron bars on the windows, which gave it the air of a prison, although much better than the houses in the upper part, made of aluminum sheets and cardboard, without running water or sewage and where everyone was extending illegal electricity pulls that the concessionaire dare not cut or charge.

Right next door, the lower part of Rocinha, where the house he was looking for is located, the luxurious condominiums of São Conrado, with swimming pools, private security and luxury cars parked in their own garage, are the symbol of the greatest social inequality in Brazil.

A young man with a feminine appearance opened the door, in fact, dressed as a woman but unable to disguise his masculine features. He introduced himself as Djamira. He had a friendly air, but a sad look. Young mulatto, perhaps 20 years old, with big eyes and thick, painted lips, giving him a supposedly seductive air, which seemed very artificial to Odacir.

Then another young man appeared, black with a similar appearance, perhaps a little younger, also wearing feminine clothes, who introduced himself as Samara, who, like the other, displayed an undisguised masculine status, from the lowest social stratum.

Immediately, Odacir realized that the two people lived in a different world from his own, that although he was also of humble origins, the fact that he had studied placed him on another social level, which did not impress him nor did it bother him, the fact that they are transvestites.

In any case, he was pleased to discover that in Rio, they can publicly display their tendencies, as it would not be possible in Parintins. Being satisfied with the room allocated to him, he closed the deal, paying a month in advance.

Within a few days, Odacir found work, temporary as it was, at a Mac Donnald's on Avenida Atlântida, on the condition that he only worked the day shift, leaving the nights free for studies.

The work at the cafeteria was a lot, he didn't get paid for overtime, but it made up for the advantage of having two free meals a day, one on arrival and the other on departure. The salary was low, but enough to pay the rent and the monthly fee for the Technical Tour Guide Course, which lasted three semesters.

He spent very little time at home, just enough to sleep and once a week to wash clothes and iron.

Once, while he was at home on his weekly rest day, he was surprised by a pitched battle between the police and members of the army, against drug traffickers who dominate the favela. The police and military forces were met with gunfire, and the day ended with the death of five criminals, there were several injuries among the forces of order and life continued as before. Everything normal. Every now and then it happened.

One day, Odacir found Djamira and Samara very excited. They were waiting for the arrival of the bomber who was going to inject them with silicone in their chests and buttocks to gain feminine shapes and thus have more demand for their activity as street prostitutes as transvestites. Odacir, who was well informed on the subject, with everything he read on Google, asked if they knew the risks they were taking.

Yes, they had already heard that there were cases of silicone spreading throughout the body, becoming deformed. From what was said on the street, Odacir tried to explain to them that the best thing to do was to start with hormonal treatments, which can be done in a public hospital. The application of surgical silicone, performed by specialized surgeons in private clinics and also in public hospitals, was one thing, and the application of industrial silicone, performed by ignorant pumpers, was another.

What they use is industrial silicone, which is very cheap but is used to clean cars and airplane parts, waterproof tiles and seal glass, cracks and holes.

While a surgeon never applies more than 500 milliliters of surgical silicone, pumpers apply liters and liters if their clients so desire. There are known cases of accumulation of more than 10 liters in people who want to have huge breasts and a huge ass. The "pumping" is done with very thick needles that make the operation extremely painful, with up to 300 punctures being made, leaving holes in the skin so large that they need to be covered with glue and nail polish. Samara didn't want to hear any more arguments from Odacir against the bomber's visit.

- You don't know half of our lives. You say that because you're educated, but I, who was thrown out on the street by my father when I was thirteen and found out that I was bullied at school for being a "faggot", had to find a way to survive. Without an education and without any possible job, what was I left to do? I ran away from Paracatu, Minas Gerais, hit the road, and hitchhiked with a truck driver who took me to Rio. During the 900-kilometer journey, the truck driver stopped three times to charge me. I had to make it

up   to   him.
With what we earn on the street, how can we afford a private doctor? And in public hospitals, full of rules, how long will hormone treatment last? We need to improve our lives today, not in a few years. We need to feel beautiful today. We risk everything for beauty and a better life.

Iracema is now sixty years old but looks much older. Life could not have been more ungrateful for the then 18-year-old girl who was admitted to the Hospital Colónia de Barbacena in the state of Minas Gerais to be cured of homosexuality. During the military dictatorship, from 1964 to 1985, the Hospital Colónia, in reality something similar to a Nazi concentration camp, was used with the supposed purpose of curing mental illnesses, sexual disorders, homosexuality, prostitution, epilepsy, alcoholism, women whose virginity had been lost before marriage, along with enemies of the political elite and socially inadequate people according to the norms of successive military governments.

Only after the fall of the military dictatorship in 1985, due to pressure from public opinion, did it become known that 70% of the patients had never suffered from any mental illness and that 60,000 people had died there, victims of mistreatment, malnutrition, electric shock "therapy" and even murder. A large percentage were black.

Iracema, a black woman, was one of the survivors of the final period of the Hospital Colónia. She was not cured. She remained an openly lesbian for the rest of her life, but the experience aged her prematurely. She currently earns her living as the most famous bombshell in Rio. She is very popular, responding every day to requests from transvestites in the largest favelas: Mangueira, Complexo do Lucas, Complexo do Alemão, Rocinha, Cidade de Deus, Maré, Jacarezinho.

She has thousands of "beauty treatments" (as she calls them) on her resume, worthy of the best reviews from her vast clientele.

For her daily commute, she has a 1979 Beetle, driven by the henchman Irineu, who, in addition to being a driver, is a gunman and bodyguard, essential to protecting her from the many who know that after each treatment she   carries   money.
She is eagerly welcomed into the home of Djamira and Samara, who see her as a saving angel.

2013

Rio de Janeiro

Dorival De Angelis, thanks to the many contacts with Brazilian high society that he has cultivated since the time he accompanied his late mother to the most popular parties, became a constant presence in the pink press due to the columns he wrote as a social critic, the occupation he adopted for himself, not because he needed to work, since his mother had left him well provided for, but because of the feeling of power that came from being flattered and feared by all those who wanted to shine in the high circle of well-to-do parties.

No one, including bankers, industrialists, politicians, artists, millionaires, those who cannot spare the permanent attention of the most frivolous but very popular press, would dare organize a gala or charity dinner, a party for the cream of high society, without previously inviting De Angelis for an appreciation of the guest list.

If he reported that so-and-so had already gone to two parties with the same Louboutin shoes, or the same Gucci bag, the same Versace accessories, or was even wearing the old Yves Saint Laurent dress from 20 years ago, the host would immediately cross her out of the guest list; if he knew that so-and-so's business was going badly and was on the verge of bankruptcy, or if someone else had a case in court due to suspicions of corruption and money laundering, no one dared to have such people as guests.

De Angelis was feared for having already caused real scandals among the most untouchables, in his famous columns of social criticism, or cast an anathema on the hosts themselves, by informing the general public that the party had lost its luster for having in its midst, inconvenient people. Those who organize parties that want to see a lot of success and are the target of De Angelis' most glowing reviews, don't invite whoever they want, they invite whoever he thinks is appropriate.

Odacir is already finishing the Tourist Guide Technical Course. He continues to work at Mac Donnald's but as soon as he finishes his course, he intends to look for another job in the tourism sector, as soon as possible, accompanying tourists on trips abroad. It would be the realization of your dream of traveling, getting to know other countries, other people, other cultures.

One day when he finished work at the snack bar, walking along Avenida Atlântida to catch the bus to Rocinha, Odacir came across a scene, unfortunately vulgar, of a group of four boys between 12 and 16 years old who surrounded a very well dressed man, they placed him against the wall of a building, and the oldest pointed a dagger at his stomach, shouting for him to give them his watch and wallet.

Odacir decided to intervene, in a placating attempt to convince the boys to let go the man and leave.

The oldest boy, undoubtedly the leader of the gang, felt the need to demonstrate his leadership of the group, and to impose his authority:

- What do you want, man? Do you want to take the pageu in the belly? And he advanced to attack him.

With a speed that didn't even make it possible to realize what had happened, the boy's armed arm was contorted in a position that if Odacir forced it, it would break and he took the weapon from his hand without difficulty.

Odacir released him, with the order to leave. The four of them ran, crossing the avenue through the heavy traffic, to take refuge on the beach.

The well-dressed gentleman, impressed by what he had seen and still scared by the attempted robbery he had been the target of, headed towards Odacir.

- Boy, you saved me. I don't even know what would have happened to me if you didn't show up. How should I thank you?

- There's nothing to thank me for. Anyway, I couldn't pass by and whistle to the side.

The one who should be thanking me was the kid I stopped from doing something stupid that could cost him for the rest of his life. But he won't recognize it. He will get another gun and continue doing the same until he is arrested. Underdog! I feel sorry for these people who seem unable to escape a tragic fate.

- Don't you want to drink anything? At least we can sit there, on that terrace and drink something, to see if I calm down.

- All right.

- What's your name, young man?

- Odacir Kauê.

- Kauê? I never heard.

- It is an indigenous name, of Tupi-Guarani origin, which is a variant of the name Kauã, which means "hawk". There is another theory according to which the name derives from the word cauê, which is a typical greeting of the Tupi people that can mean either "hail" or "kind man".

- Curious! Kind man. I think the name suits you perfectly.

- And what is your name, sir?

- Dorival De Angelis, at your service, with my thanks. But please don't call me sir. I'm not that old yet.

- Of course, Dorival. You're not old at all. You're a little over 30, aren't you?

- 35. And you?

- 21.

Odacir didn't say so, but he thought that Dorival was quite charming and very pleasant.

While they had a beer and a little catupiri, the conversation progressed affably, allowing each one to introduce themselves informally, telling what they did and how they made a living. Meanwhile, Dorival discreetly observed the young Odacir, delighting in the contemplation of his semi-wild beauty that his indigenous origins gave to his slightly dark skin.

- My dear Odacir, I once created a lot of men's clothing, which I didn't sell and I don't even know what to do with. I can provide you some better clothes, I might even help you to find a job in the new profession you want to pursue. Would you like to come to my house and see if anything fits you? I live very close by, in this avenue.

- If you don't know what to do with the clothes, then very well, I thank you.

Odacir only left Dorival's house the next morning to go to work.

Not only did he gain a varied wardrobe of designer clothes that he never imagined he would be able to wear, but he had also gained a friend, a lover and a protector.

2014

Rio de Janeiro

Truly in love with his new boyfriend, Dorival insisted a lot on Odacir to stop sharing the house in Rocinha and move in to live with him in Avenida Atlântida.

For Odacir, moving to Dorival's house meant a radical change in his way of life and social status. He left behind the squalor, insecurity and penury of a society eternally condemned to a painful survival, to enjoy unexpected wealth and the paternalistic protection of her wealthy boyfriend, who set out, as a short-term project, to polish the edges of the diamond. in the rough that was his "little Indian".

In all aspects of his daily life, Odacir was the target of Dorival's most attentive intervention, in order to correct him and educate him for his new life in an environment of high society.

From the way of dressing and combing the hair, to the choice of clothes and footwear, to etiquette and table manners, in the way of speaking, including popular expressions to avoid, more typical of an indigenous language than of an erudite verbalization, which Odacir gladly accepted, assuming that it was progress in his education from humble beginnings.

His reference became the book "Savoir Faire", by Maitê Avelar De Angelis, the still famous, although deceased mother of Dorival, the etiquette manual recognized as the "Bible" in Brazilian high society.

Complementing his training as a debutante in high society, Dorival began taking his pupil to exhibitions in art galleries, to cultural events and to theater shows, new experiences that aroused a great interest in him.

Six months of intense preparation were necessary for Dorival to consider that young Odacir was prepared to be introduced to society but, before he did so, there would be a need to build a life history for Odacir, hiding his origins as a humble fisherman from the Amazon.

Then the first disagreement between them arose. If for Dorival, it was necessary for his protégé to be presented as coming from a family with a good social reputation, educated in good schools, for Odacir, this was absolutely unacceptable. For two reasons: firstly, because he had no reason to be ashamed of his origins and, secondly, because he would be easily unmasked if he presented himself with a false life.

It was because he recognized the danger of this happening that Dorival allowed Odacir to say he was born in Parintins, avoiding divulging what his parents did, but reinforcing the importance of having been educated at a prestigious religious school, what always goes well, as a resume. Meanwhile, it was necessary to find a profession for Odacir, more worthy than an assistant at a lunch bar.

Once he had already finished the Travel Guide Technical Course, he had to find a job to practice a new profession.

Thanks to his many contacts, Dorival managed to get an interview at Flytours for Odacir, where he was admitted and went on to do a training internship.

His first trips accompanying foreign tourists were to Foz do Iguaçu, Fortaleza, Recife and Salvador. After a year of experience with national packages, he will start accompanying excursionists abroad, which is what interests him most.

Odacir began to accompany Dorival to parties, gala dinners, cocktail parties and charity teas that he attended as a social critic.
Odacir was well accepted by society, which saw him as a friendly, educated young man interested in cultural issues. However, just like his life experience had taught him, he could not help but feel that, behind the complacency of convenience with which he was accepted by everyone, certainly to get into Dorival's good graces, some of these people were unable to hide a never-verbalized expression of superiority with which he looked at, a mestizo, who, although his skin was practically white, his features showed an ancestral ethnic origin.

Never before, in his restricted circles of relationships within his social stratum, had he felt the target of any type of racism, but now, among white people from high society, although they treated him cordially, he felt the discomfort of being looked at by some as an inferior one, although no one has ever expressed it. It was something he felt, even though he was never the target of even the slightest racist remark.

He decided to hide his discomfort about this situation, not only because he had felt it from a minority of the people he had met, but also because he didn't want to bother Dorival with such a subject. A person learns to live with these people, despising them. The truth was that the mundane social life at that level of high society, however glamorous it was, disappointed him a little.

Odacir had other concerns in mind, much more pressing than facing the looks of superiority from part of his social contacts, which he began to respond with disdain.

He had been feeling the need to express the feminine side of his biological and mental identity, but he understood that, from the moment he would undergo hormonal treatments, such as silicone implants to gain very feminine breasts and buttocks, from the moment he would use makeup and dress like a woman, he would lose his job immediately and probably wouldn't find anyone who would give him a job again.

For him, losing the right to work was unthinkable. He didn't want to live in eternal dependence on Dorival.

One day, to find out Dorival's feelings on the subject, he asked if he could love a man with a woman's body and dressed as a woman.

- But does the guy have a penis, or has he already cut it? – the boyfriend replied, amused.

- No, consider one with a penis.

- In a woman's body? If I liked women, may be, but I don't, so, for me, with a woman's body, it would not be possible.

2015-2018

Rio de Janeiro

Odacir's desire to transform his body, acquiring feminine forms, has been successively postponed for the most diverse reasons, first, at school, to avoid being bullied, then, to avoid revealing his gender orientation to his father and to Parintins society, and, more recently, to be able to finish a course in Rio de Janeiro and keep a job. He is afraid he will never be free from the intolerance he expects to suffer if he came out.

He has reached his limit of self-restraint, repressing his true nature that demanded to assert himself, when his boyfriend Dorival did not recognize this right.

From that day on, although he had not expressed it, this attitude gradually began to provoke in Odacir a resentment that led to a latent feeling of distance and loss of affection. Dorival, understanding the signs of Odacir's withdrawal and trying to do everything he could to not lose him, thought he could lift his spirits by taking him to more parties where he could meet interesting people who would make him feel good and give him more joy in life.

However, Odacir, although he liked Dorival, could not continue to accept his rejection of the idea of transforming his body and acquiring, as had been his old ambition, to become a woman.

He decided that the invitation to go to a banquet at the Consulate General of Portugal would be the last one he would go to with him and after that, he would separate from Dorival, although he wanted to continue to see him as the great friend that he really was.

The São Clemente Palace, located in the Botafogo neighborhood, was built in the 1950s to be the headquarters of the Portuguese Embassy in

Brazil. With the capital's move to Brasília, the building began to be used as the official residence of the Portuguese Consul of Rio de Janeiro.

The work of Portuguese architect Guilherme Rebelo de Andrade, best known for being the designer of the Luminous Fountain on Alameda Dom Afonso Henriques in Lisbon, was built on a total area of almost 6,000 square metres, including a large and leafy garden.

The Palace was built with fine materials brought from Portugal, such as marble from Extremoz, tile panels from the Fábrica da Viúva Lamego, tapestries from Arraiolos and classical furniture from the Ricardo Espírito Santo Foundation. Inside, a 17th-century Baroque chapel was reconstructed, brought from Portugal.

The current Consul Henrique Athaíde de Lencastre is a 40-year-old bachelor, grandson of a career diplomat who had been Portugal's Ambassador to India before the loss of Goa, Daman and Diu in 1961. His father, already retired, had also been Ambassador to Italy, Germany and Switzerland. The young Henrique, who had accompanied his father on this journey, had become a polyglot, fluent in Italian, German, French and English. Heir to the family's diplomatic vein, he graduated in International Relations and Political and Economic Diplomacy at the Lusófona University in Porto.

After completing his degree, he joined the Ministry of Foreign Affairs and was posted to Rio de Janeiro as the Consul General of Portugal.

At a time when Odacir had already decided to live alone in an apartment in Barra da Tijuca, close to his workplace, the headquarters of Fly Tours, from where the excursions to accompany tourists departed, he and Dorival continued to have a friendly relationship, and from time to time, they would go together to cocktail parties and society parties.

The Consulate General of Portugal in Rio de Janeiro maintains the tradition of celebrating Portugal Day, Camões Day and the Portuguese Communities Day every year on the 10th June.

Because the Consul wanted to guarantee coverage of the event in the written and television press, Dorival was one of the guests and took Odacir with him to a cocktail party, followed by dinner, in the grand hall of the São Clemente Palace.

They had avoided the ceremonies and speeches for the official guests who took place during the afternoon, at the Royal Portuguese Reading Cabinet, the magnificent Portuguese library, one of the most beautiful in the world, installed in a building built for this purpose, in neo-Manueline style, reminiscent of the Jerónimos Monastery, on Rua Luís de Camões, Rio de Janeiro, inaugurated in 1887.

The dinner has been served at the São Clemente Palace, for a smaller group of guests, just fifty, included Portuguese personalities, prominent in Brazilian society, bankers, intellectuals, journalists, artists, major industrialists and traders.

After dinner, which took place with the informality of someone who had known each other for a long time, while most of the guests went out to the terrace to smoke and enjoy the lighting of the leafy garden, Odacir did not fail to appreciate the decorative faiences by Raphael Bordalo Pinheiro and the Marinha Grande glass sculptures that adorned the shelves of the main hall, on whose walls precious paintings by José Malhoa, Carlos Reis, Eduardo Malta and Henrique Medina were displayed.

Odacir was enjoying a Malhoa, with a glass of Porto in his hand, when a voice surprised him beside him:

- José Malhoa, my favorite.

It was the Consul who spoke to him.

- Are you a journalist, a colleague of Dorival De Angelis?

- No, I'm not a journalist. I'm just his friend.

In a brief exchange of looks that spoke more than words, as if they were codes of silence, they both realized that there was something that brought them together and it wasn't difficult for them to understand what it was.

The Consul invited Odacir to visit him soon, to get to know each other better.

Their meetings resulted in the discovery of a mutual, overwhelming passion that justified a de facto union. Less than a month later they met for the first time, and after three meetings with the Consul, Odacir has been invited to live at the São Clemente Palace.

In the second month of his stay at the Palace, continuing to practice his profession, Odacir found it necessary to address with his lover the essential and unavoidable for him, issue of becoming a woman.

Henrique was open to the idea, without any problems, as long as Odacir promised that he would not perform surgery to remove the penis and "fabricate" a vagina.

- No, that was never my idea. What I want is to gain feminine features and body and dress like a woman. But no surgeries.

- In this case, count on me to support you and pay all the expenses inherent to the transformation, hormonal treatments and silicone implants to be carried out exclusively in a responsible clinic with a scientific reputation. No ignorant and unconscious bombers.

It was impressive what the clinicians managed to do, in a surprising hormonal process of applying estrogens and anti-androgens that lasted two years, resulting in voluminous and perfect breasts, wide hips, accentuated waist, sensual, slightly prominent lips, absence of hair in the body and a progressive feminization of the features and even the voice, with notable changes, not only in the lips, but also in the apples of the cheeks, in the eyebrows, in the forehead and in the long hair that he began to wear. The final result of a symbiosis between natural origin and scientific creation was the stunning figure of a beautiful woman, with a perfect body, awakening lustful desires, not only in men, but also in women, especially if they were able to guess what he kept between his legs.

Having already officially approved same-sex marriage in Brazil, Odacir and Henrique got married, in a discreet and intimate ceremony, in front of a small number of friends, of which Dorival was part, but the press did not echo this.

Odacir stopped working at the travel agency and, now transformed, began accompanying her husband to all official ceremonies, for convenient protocol purposes.

Her extreme feminine beauty was evident, an example of refined elegance and good taste, in which no one would detect a masculine origin.

They lived an intense and honest relationship until misfortune revealed liver cancer to Henrique, which killed him in just three months of unbearable suffering.

53

PORTUGAL

2022

Expresso newspaper. Lisbon

Laura Sobral enjoys prestige in the editorial office of the weekly Expresso that allows her to select the topics she decides to write about and sometimes carry out long periods of intense research and analysis.

Her reputation as an investigative journalist among his colleagues, his editor-in-chief, Artur Varela, the newspaper's owner and founder, Francisco Balsemão, and even the Journalists Union, began to be cemented soon after her admission to the newspaper, after finishing her degree in Communication and Journalism when, on her own initiative, she developed an investigation into the arrests of alleged terrorists by the CIA, in reaction to the attack on the Twin Towers, on September 11, 2001.

Her investigations led to the writing of an extensive article that denounced the imprisonment of at least 136 individuals in secret CIA prisons in 54 countries, including Syria, Egypt, Jordan, Macedonia, Libya, Lithuania, Morocco, Romania, Thailand and Afghanistan.

The article that mentioned one by one the names of several people detained in inhumane circumstances and subjected to torture approved by the Bush administration as "enhanced interrogation techniques", that included being naked and suspended for days and nights by the wrists, the sleep deprivation, drowning, subjection to starvation, the use of a chair designed to stretch the spine, and suspension by hands tied behind the back that causes the shoulders to dislocate, just as it was done in the Middle Ages.

The CIA inspectors themselves concluded that in some cases, the detainees had no connection to terrorism and that only their names were similar to those of others being persecuted.

The article ended up being sold to several foreign newspapers, which gained great credibility for the then young journalist.

Over her almost 20-year career, she has authored numerous investigations in collaboration with the ICIJ - International Consortium of Investigating Journalists, a group of 280 journalists in 100 countries and with the EIC - European Investigative Collaborations, the joining of efforts of several European newspapers and television stations.

The newspaper Expresso is part of both organizations and published articles written by Laura Sobral about the Panama Papers, Isabel dos Santos' fortune and corruption in Angola, former prime minister José Sócrates, the war in Afghanistan, the history of the Russian feminist group, Pussy Riot, the freedom of expression in Hungary, the meteoric rise of the Chinese city of Shenzhen, the reconstruction of Kosovo, the persecuted citizens of Iran, the integration of Portuguese military personnel into the forces of the Nations United Nations in the Central African Republic, rapes by UN soldiers in Haiti, the Central African Republic, the Democratic Republic of Congo, South Sudan, Bosnia and Kosovo and the disappearance of children in Portugal.

Divorced, without children, Laura is available to take care of herself. She can't do without a weekly trip to a beauty center to take care of her hair and nails and have her skin cleaned.

Three times a week, in a gym close to home, she practices fitness with strength, cardio, coordination and flexibility exercises, resulting in an athletic, healthy complexion and a look of impeccable elegance that gives her a much younger appearance and makes her the target of libidinous glances from many men she meets. With all due respect and friendship, her friend and editor-in-chief, Artur Varela, had already defined her, in conversation with colleagues, that she has the sensual mouth of Angelina Jolie, the perfect little nose of Nicole Kidman, and the toned body and sensuality by Jennifer Lopez. Everyone finds it strange that she continues to live alone and no one knows her any lovers, just occasional weekend outings with colleagues and friends for dinner and drinks.

Her positive attitude towards life, her permanent good disposition and affability in human relationships make her a well-liked person by everyone she comes into contact with.

She is thinking about an upcoming research project that she wants to discuss first with Artur, also a senior member of the ICIJ and journalist with an internationally recognized CV, author of several highly successful books. In the editor-in-chief's office, Laura decided to present the idea to her friend:

- Arthur, I'm thinking about a question that aroused my curiosity recently. Accustomed to sticking my nose into everything, I have long noticed the number of transvestites offering their services in Correio da Manhã social ads. Everyone knows they exist but I had no idea there could be so many. Based on the logic that if they exist and advertise themselves it is because they have customers and there is a functioning market, I decided to gather more information on the subject and discovered several websites on the Internet, above all, a very well done one, where I was surprised by a large number of "them", with many good quality photographs, showing perfect female bodies, many beautiful faces, well combed and well made-up, in provocative lingerie and full nudes, each "one" displaying a respectable member between the legs, whose measures are indicated and will make many men ashamed and envious. They are advertised throughout the country, even in smaller cities and the most curious thing is that more than 95% of "them" are Brazilian, which led me to look for other information in Brazil.

I was very shocked when I discovered several articles and even undergraduate theses in PDF where they mentioned that the life expectancy of a transsexual in Brazil is only 35 years! This is because they are the target of savage persecution, suffering torture and murder or ending up committing suicide. This is very serious and gives food for thought.

Don't you think it's worth doing a study on this, an authentic social phenomenon?

- Yeah, I had no idea. Mainly because they come here in such numbers, and the general public, like me, doesn't think they know the true extent of what is happening, it's worth delving deeper into the subject. However, what superficially seems to me to be just a variant of homosexuality, in today's Europe, talking about gays no longer sells newspapers.

In general, or at least in much of Europe, homosexuality is viewed by society with much greater tolerance than in the past and accepted to the point where several countries now officially recognize same-sex marriage. Now, a politician who publicly reveals his homosexuality, which no one knew about, even gains points in voter acceptance. So as long as your work isn't specifically about homosexuality, which no one else cares about, then I guess, go ahead with the idea.

- You're right, but anyway, as an introduction to the subject, because many people still think that homosexuality is a thing of modernity, the result of a time in which a large part of moral values is lost, and debauchery reigns, I think it will be interesting, to reveal, as a historical curiosity, how homosexuality was seen in the past.

- Okay. All good. You really like explaining the roots of issues.

- You know very well that no one understands the present if they don't know the past.

- Show me what you write about this. I'm also curious. It's a subject I ignore because it never interested me.

2022

Expresso newspaper. Lisbon

- Arthur - to satisfy your curiosity, I bring here the introduction I wrote about homosexuality throughout the history of humanity. It was fun to discover certain things.

I leave you the text on this pen. Then you tell me what you think.

"Many people think that civil unions between people of the same sex are an aberration of modern societies, which in the past, the preservation of traditional values would never allow.

Only due to ignorance of the historical truth can one think like this. It is not true that gay marriage, now officially recognized in more than 20 countries, is a foreign idea to ancestral societies, simply because in some ancient peoples the concept of homosexuality did not even exist.

The oldest knowledge on the subject dates back to around 10,000 years ago, in some Melanesian tribes in the Pacific, today the Solomon Islands, Fiji and New Guinea, where sexual intercourse between two men, one of them dressed as a woman, was a ritual of a religious nature to achieve sacred knowledge.

Around 1750 bC in ancient Mesopotamia, one of the oldest codes of law in the world, the Code of King Hammurabi, which recognized privileges attributed to prostitutes and prostitutes who participated in sacred rituals. Such sacred relationships between pairs of devout men or women were practiced in temples not only in Mesopotamia but also in Phoenicia, Egypt, India and even closer to us, in Sicily.

The Hittite laws, heirs to the Code of Hammurabi, from more than 3,000 years ago, recognized the union between people of the same sex in the Turkish region of Anatolia and in parts of present-day Syria and Lebanon.

The great conqueror Alexander the Great (356-323 bC) had as a lover, Hephastion, who held a high position in his army.

The Greek philosopher Socrates (470-399 bC) defended homosexual love and preached that anal intercourse was the best form of inspiration, declaring that heterosexual intercourse was only justified for procreation. It was not just the personal opinion of someone who today would be considered an open homosexual, but it simply reflected a widespread way of thinking in ancient Greece and Rome, where it was absolutely normal for a man to have sexual relations with a younger man.

It was part of the education of young Athenians between 12 and 18 years old, to accept being, as passive pupils, and with the approval of their family, the friendship and love of older men to absorb their virtues and knowledge of Philosophy. Only at the age of 25 did they become men and began to have a role that was assumed to be active with a young man, but they were not allowed to have relationships with other adults, since society viewed passive elements as unworthy and they were even prevented from exercising public positions and being relegated to a lower social status than slaves. However, among the great and powerful, their own will imposed itself on the current codes.

The Roman writer Suetonius stated in the book "The Lives of the Twelve Caesars" that only one of them, Claudius, never had sexual relations with other men. Julius Caesar (100-44 bC) had a relationship with Nicomedes, king of Bithynia, in Asia Minor, an ally of Rome.

Among them, the most eccentric were Caligula (12-41 aD) who forced his subjects to kiss his penis and Nero (37-68 aD) who had two husbands and had relations with his own mother.

In Greek and Roman mythology and also in Babylon and India, homosexuality existed among their gods, which, naturally, was a divine reference for humanity. For example, the Hindu god Ganesh would have been born from the union between two female deities.

Religions have always influenced and normalized ideas about sexual practices. The life of humanity passed under laws that reflected divine beliefs. With Judaism, the widespread idea about the normality of sexual practices came from God's demand "Grow and multiply".

After a long period in which worshipers of Jesus were persecuted in the Roman Empire for not worshiping the emperor, in the year 380, by edict of Emperor Theodosius I, Christianity became the official religion of the entire empire and, since then, homosexuality came to be considered unnatural and subject to repression.

Much later, during the Renaissance humanism, poets, painters and sculptors revived the cult of antiquity for the male form. Some of the nobility made homosexuality fashionable, practiced without censorship or restrictions. King Richard the Lionheart (1157-1199) became known as a homosexual, having had a love affair with Philip II, King of France.

Leonardo Da Vinci had at least two male companions throughout his life, and was never ashamed of it. His portraits of his boyfriend Salai are part of his historical legacy.

Michelangelo maintained a very discreet private life, but there were reports that the painter was gay. Tommaso de Cavalieri, considered a man of sublime beauty, is said to have aroused an intense passion in the painter in 1532. Benedetto Varchi, an Italian historian and poet, was another suspect. Pietro Aretino, a painter, was the most suspicious. Was it simply envy of his competitor?

Several other European monarchs, such as Henry III of France (1551-1529) and James IV of Scotland and I of England, had several lovers. But it was not just the kings. For the nobles of the court, it was simply a matter of imitating the kings.

The Queen of France, Marie Antoinette (1755-1793), certainly as a result of her husband's impotence, indulged in a variety of sexual relations with men and women, including the Princess of Lamballe, her brother-in-law, the Count d'Artois and the Swedish Count Hans Fersen.

Between 1347 and 1351, the Black Death swept through Europe, killing 25 million people. In the absence of a scientific explanation for its causes, the Church, with the easy acquiescence of popular ignorance, blamed the calamity on unnatural practices, homosexuals and, while we're at it, on Jews and heretics, who suffered persecution and massacres in many parts of Europe. From the 16th century onwards, the Inquisition began to investigate, judge and condemn sodomy to the stake.

A pair of researchers, after a meticulous analysis of 182 sonnets by the playwright Shakespeare, claim that there is unquestionable evidence that the Englishman was bisexual. The Sodomy Statute Chapter 17, which was approved by the English Parliament in 1562, stated that sexual acts between men should be punished.

Also in the 19th century, citizens accused of sodomy, anal intercourse, with either a man or a woman, were hanged in England.

The famous Irish poet, playwriter Oscar Wilde was sentenced in 1895 for "sexual crimes" to two and a half years in prison and hard labor. Famous American film actors and actresses have lived lives filled with bisexual relationships, such as Marlon Brando, Greta Garbo, Katharine Hepburn, Joan Crawford, and Judy Garland.

The famous dancer Isadora Duncan and jazz singer Billie Halliday were also openly bisexual.

The Englishman Alan Turing, the famous mathematician, computer scientist, and cryptanalyst, to whom not only England but the entire world owed the acceleration of the end of the Second World War, when his team managed to decode the encrypted messages of the German Enigma machine, which for a long time gave control of the Atlantic to German submarines that destroyed American and English ships loaded with US supplies, was sentenced to be chemically castrated in replacement of prison, in 1952, for "homosexual activity". Only in 2013 did England grant him a "posthumous pardon".

The most famous and most beloved Spanish poet, Frederico Garcia Lorca, whose works were censored for hiding his sexuality, suffered persecution for something that neither he nor his family ever recognized. Letters were found that linked him to Salvador Dali. In 1936, Lorca was murdered by Spanish fascists, "for homosexual and abnormal practices".

The Portuguese neurosurgeon, António Egas Moniz, was awarded the Nobel Prize for Medicine in 1949, for his invention and practice of lobotomy, a surgical technique that began to be adopted in many countries, which consisted of cutting a piece of the brain of mentally ill people, severe cases of schizophrenia but there were also doctors who used it to "cure" homosexuals and nymphomaniac women. 3,000 gay men were lobotomized in Sweden, 3,500 in Denmark, by 1981.

At the time, homosexuality was still considered a disease and in the United States around 50 thousand citizens were lobotomized, some of them carriers of the then scientifically considered genetic defect "sexual dysfunctions".

The surgery resulted in 6% deaths and the transformation of troublesome mentally ill patients into peaceful vegetative states. Today, Egas Moniz would be considered one of the greatest murderers in the history of medicine, along with Josef Mengele, the doctor who carried out terrifying experiments on prisoners in the Auschwitz concentration camp.

In 1979, the American Psychiatric Association finally removed homosexuality from the list of mental illnesses and in 2004 the United States Supreme Court

invalidated all laws that criminalized homosexuality and prohibited discrimination against gays and lesbians.

The World Health Organization - WHO, excluded homosexuality as a mental illness in 1990, which it rectified only in 1992.

In Portugal, in 2010, the Assembly of the Republic legalized same-sex marriage and in 2015 legalized adoption by same-sex couples.

The WHO removed transsexuality from the list of mental illnesses in 2018, which removes the justification for the supposed treatments and cures that were being practiced and which are now considered disrespectful to the sexual diversity of human beings.

The document was officially approved in 2019 and only came into force on January 1th, 2022".

2022

Lisbon

Savoy and Joaquim are a couple of Brazilian visual artists who, in addition to living together, both work at home, each on their own art.

Savoy is a painter and Joaquim does everything his imagination asks of him, with any type of material, but especially with wood, as in his youth, he had been a carpenter as his first profession, in his native Bahia. In addition to his varied works in wood, he produces sculptures in recycled metals, plasters, fabrics and papers that he makes himself.

Lately, they have specialized in recycling furniture abandoned in the trash that they restore giving it a new and surprising look that gives it a new useful and decorative life or just as a work of contemporary art, merely contemplative. This couple's imagination and creativity have no limits. Currently they have an exhibition of chairs recovered from the trash, transformed into surprising sculptures displayed on a wall at Palácio Quintela, in Chiado, the headquarters of IADE, the Institute of Art and Decoration. At the opening alone, almost all of them were sold.

Either one or the other survives through some occasional work for advertising campaigns and what they sell at exhibitions, or in art galleries, or in their own residence, in a Pombaline building next to the Cathedral, which is often the stage for cultural evenings on Saturdays, sometimes with musicians, singers or poem readers, as well as exhibitions and sales of works by other artists, mostly Brazilian and gay, a very eclectic community that brings together some intellectually interesting personalities.

The two were lovers for many years but ended their relationship and decided to have their sex life separately, although the solid friendship that unites them, and the advantage of complementing each other in some work together, prevents a physical separation, so they will continue, in principle forever, living and working in the same house.

Savoy's new boyfriend is Carlinhos, Portuguese, working and living in Santiago do Cacém. He comes to Lisbon every weekend to be with Savoy. Joaquim accepts his presence at home quite naturally. Everyone lives together in the greatest harmony and friendship.

Laura has maintained a friendly relationship with Savoy and Joaquim for years. She was always invited to the opening of their exhibitions and to cultural evenings at their house. Sometimes, some of the pieces that don't sell are offered to her and the decoration of her home today is already a sampling of their works.

With some frequency, either Laura will have dinner at their house or they will have dinner at her house. They are always good company and have evenings in the best family atmosphere. At their home, they showcase the best Brazilian specialties. Joaquim is a skilled cook and surprises Laura with the best cuisine from the Brazilian Northeast: Moqueca Capixaba, Acarajé, Tacacá, Vatapá and when they bring dried meat, he makes Paçoca do Piaui and Feijoada with kale from Minas Gerais.

Knowing that Brazilians love cod, Laura always makes a different dish for them. It's still a long way from reaching the traditional 100 ways to cook the "faithful friend", as it is called in Portugal.

Over the years of living together, Laura developed a very complicit attitude towards them, as well as with other gay friends. They are amused when she starts conversations with "Let's talk about our men". They all open up to her in the greatest intimacy, as if they were in the confessional. In the end, everyone laughs a lot and drink another glass of red wine.

- My dears. I invited you to come here today because I'm going to start a project, for which I'll need your initial help.

I intend to do an investigation into the lives of transsexuals, women and men. I learned that a large number of transsexuals pass through Portugal dedicated to the sex business. I have seen countless advertisements on the Internet that show beautiful faces, perfect female bodies, worthy of beauty contests, but with a "surprise bonus", a penis, some of an enviable size. If it were just for the discovery of this reality, I wouldn't even be interested in developing a journalistic work on the subject, but what caught my attention was discovering that in Brazil, they are persecuted, tortured and even murdered, with complete impunity. Prevented by society's prejudices from working in any profession, the only way out is to embrace prostitution and many end up committing suicide, to the point that their life expectancy in Brazil is reduced to 35 years, which I found to be a scandal and a national shame. That's why I decided to intervene, to denounce the prejudices and practices that violate human rights against these people, who are people like the rest of us. I remembered that perhaps you know or are friends with someone in this environment, a man or a woman who does not identify with the sex with which they were born. I want to meet them, interview them, to try to get society to understand and accept them in the same way that the gay and lesbian communities are accepted today. At least that, so that they stop being victims of criminal violence.

- Well, said Savoy, always more involved in socially oriented dialogues. Being accepted and understood, even in Portugal, is still relative. While it is true that the right to same-sex marriage and adoption of children is already recognized, the truth is that there are still many complexes in the minds of many more conservative or religious people who do not agree with these official decisions. But that will always be there... or maybe it will take a long time to change, – interrupted Lara, – the truth is that almost no one denies the right of gays and lesbians to practice any profession. They are accepted in any profession and by all social strata, while trans people are still at the level of the untouchable caste in India.

- Yes, Joaquim intervened: - it's true, as long as they're not exhibitionist fags, given to public vulgarity, most people no longer look at us as perverse mental patients, as they did in the past. But look, we don't know any trans people personally. It's a tribe apart, you know? But we can take you to a transvestite show one of these nights and you'll even have fun. You might meet some of them there. Talk to them after the show, and you can go drink at the fountain, added Joaquim, why don't you ask for an interview with the directors of the ILGA Portugal Association - Lesbian, Gay, Bisexual, Trans and Intersex Intervention?

They can put you in touch with some people you want to interview.

- Are you members? - No. We don't need to make a big deal about who we are. We're not part of any association - informed Savoy.

Laura couldn't help but think: - Since they are people with an absolutely normal attitude in society, if they don't say it, no one will detect any mannerisms that reveal their sexual orientation. That's why they live fully integrated with society like any other straight citizens. As always, none of them show any signs of intimacy with straight people, even if they are friends, like Laura, to respect them and not hurt their feelings, but there is something that is leaving Savoy unsatisfied.

- Excuse me, dear. Can you give me permission for Carlinhos to sit on my lap? We only see each other at the weekend and I miss him terribly.

The request, made with the touching naturalness and purity of a child, revealed only a lack of affection without, at the time, revealing any sexual connotation. They were just two human beings who needed to feel together. Without needing to say anything to them, responding only with a gesture that meant they were at ease, Laura agreed, certain that they would never kiss in her presence.

- They are so sweet, - she thought.

2022

Trumps Club. Lisbon

Because ILGA is closed during the weekend, to advance contacts in the gay and transsexual community, friends Savoy and Carlinhos took Laura to see a transformation Joaquim show, always more reserved and averse to showing what he derogatorily calls "pussy", preferred to stay at home.

For Laura, it will be a first approach to the transsexual community, to begin with, on the more fun side, apparently far from the dramas and tragedies that mark the lives of many of them.

They chose to go to Lisbon's most famous gay club, Trumps, on Rua da Imprensa Nacional, which have shows every weekend for 40 years.

- Laura, make sure you watch one or another excessive exhibitionism from some who come here to hook up – warned Savoy. You will see many guys dancing shirtless, already well drunk.

- They are not going to start having sex in public, are they?

- No, not that. Those in a hurry go to the bathroom.

- All right. We came here, to see the show. I want to try to understand, if I can, what artists' lives are like, beyond the scenes. It would be good if we found someone to introduce us to the artists. I will need to gain people's trust so that they can later confide in me about their lives. Don't you know anyone here?

- In principle, no, replied Savoy. I haven't been here, over twenty years, but I might wander around to see if I recognize anyone from other times. And you, Carlinhos, see if you know anyone here.

- Me?... who spent my life there stuck in Judas's ass, in Santiago do Cacém, who never came to a transvestite show?

Two whiskeys later, Savoy returned to the table with the information that the show is a tribute to the most famous transvestite in Portugal, the famous

Belle Dominique, who turns 72 today and is there fresh as lettuce, at a table with friends.

You certainly remember her, she was well known nationally and internationally. She performed in the best concert halls and participated in television programs. Do you remember "Minas & Armadilhas" and "Big Show Sic"?

She didn't know, because she must have still been a child, but she quickly looked up Belle Dominique on Google. There was no lack of information about the star. It became known that she had won the Best Transvestite award in 1982, from Nova Gente magazine, the Career Award, in 2009 at the Embrace Gala and Honorable Mention at the Lisbon Erotic Salon, the same year.

His real name is Domingos Machado. The person who is watching today's show is Belle Dominique, not Domingos Machado. That's why she is wearing makeup and dressed in character, with feathers and sequins, as was the tradition of her presentations.

The journalist, despite the exuberance that was striking at the artist's advanced age, seemed a little unreasonable, but she could not help but admire her pose of great security and dignity that her fame justified.

The show was very lively and culminated in an apotheosis of ovation from the noisy and excited audience that filled the room, when at the end, the honoree spoke a few words of thanked the artists and the public.

Laura waited for Belle Dominique to return to the table and introduced herself to her.

- Dear Belle Dominique, my name is Laura Sobral and I am a journalist for the newspaper Expresso. I would like to interview you, whenever and wherever is convenient for you. I am starting a research project on the transgenic community, focused on defending their rights like any other human being and not from the perspective of social, moral or ideological criticism.

- I would be very pleased. We can combine. Now I have all the time in the world.

- I will be more interested in getting to know you as Domingos Machado, the person and not the character you play.

- I understand. I'm available whenever you want.

- Excellent. Let's not meet in the newspaper office. It would be too formal. I would prefer if we met in a place where you can feel more comfortable, like a meeting between two friends.

- Very well, where do you suggest?

- At Tivoli Forum, on Avenida da Liberdade, just below the Tivoli cinema, there is a Literary Club that has a bookstore and bar. Could it be?

- Yes. When?

- Could it be next Monday at 3pm? We'll have all afternoon to talk.

- Very well, I'll be there.

2022

Literary Club. Lisbon

Whoever attended the meeting with the journalist was a completely a different person from the one Laura had met the previous week. Instead of the sophisticated female figure in a spectacular outfit, an elderly man appeared, impeccably combed and shaved, in casual but tasteful clothing, accentuating his masculine charm. A spontaneous and affectionate smile revealed, at first contact, the human nature of a simple and easy going soul.

Anyone who saw them could think they were father and daughter, so natural and affable did they prove to be, the first moments of their meeting. Laura couldn't stop thinking about the surprise caused by the total absence of mannerisms or even intonation in his voice, different from the one she already knew, that could reveal even a spark of the feminine side she had known in Trumps. In front of her was a gentleman who radiated respectability, reinforced by his white hair that gave him an aura of seductive masculinity.

They both agreed it was too early for alcoholic drinks, so they opted for tea. Later they would take something else.

- Would you allow me to record our conversation? It's so that later, I don't forget anything.

- Feel free.

Laura turned on a small pocket recorder that she placed on the table.

- I would like you to start with what was your first experience as a transvestite was. What was the atmosphere, how did you feel, what were people's reactions.

- It was in the army, in Angola. I was doing my military service and decided to take part in the Christmas show in 1973. It was the first time I wore women's clothes and created a character where I pretended to be a woman. Imagine the conservative climate of the time and an audience of Latino males. I took a big risk, but I caricatured the character so much that it resulted in a burlesque show that made everyone laugh and there were no major consequences, apart from the fact that, from then on, colleagues and superiors began to look at me in a different way and there was no shortage of malicious mockery of my sexuality. It was the price to pay for brief moments of great success as an actor.

- I imagine. And did that mark you for life?

- It has hurted me but I decided not to attach too much importance to them.

I decided that I would not allow this to affect my identity. Moving forward, no matter what they think of me. It can't be others who decide our lives, right?

- A highly positive philosophy of life, that's what I think - Laura replied.

- After completing my military service, I joined RTP, the national television channel, as a full-time employee, performing multiple tasks in production, where I had the opportunity to meet artists, technicians and directors with whom I gained trust and friendship and from whom I learned a lot about the world of spectacle. They thought I was funny and I was given opportunities to occasionally participate in some shows, in secondary roles, such as in "Christmas in hospitals".

Continuing with my job at RTP, but feeling that I was capable of greater flights as I was riding a wave of creativity, decided to do my own shows.

The character Belle Dominique was born in 1976 at Memorial Bar. The following year, at Bar Ronda, in Estoril, I created the group Travecoop and performed the shows that were hugely successful at the time, "Cabaret", "Frenéticas", "Les Poupées de Paris" and "Ovninfas of the 3th Degree", a parody to the film Encounters of the 3th degree.

- I've never heard of it. At that time, I was not born, yet.

- I was so successful that I was hired by SIC, the other TV channel, to participate in several programs there. The figure of Belle Dominique gained great popular support, in hundreds of live shows, to the point that SIC invested in presenter Júlio César's program "Minas e Armadilhas" in which I was the star. Later, with the presenter João Baião, with whom I became great friends, I participated as a jury on the "Big Show SIC" program.

- It's curious. It seems that at that time there was much greater popular acceptance of transvestite shows than there is today. Now, such spectacles are not seen on any TV channel, nor are they heard of. It is vaguely known that they continue to exist, but confined to gay bars, as far as I know.

- It's true, it is. Today there are fewer non-gay curious people going to shows which, by the way, are offensively cheap today. Can you imagine, a show like the one you saw, tickets being sold for 10 euros, including a drink?

What can artists earn?

- Has the quality of the show suffered? - Undoubtedly. It stopped being a popular show and became a show for minorities. There continue to be good artists but the production itself, given the scarcest means, had to suffer a lot.

- Why do you think it was so popular?

- Well, I think we benefited from an unusual time, in an absolutely new social and political framework. After the conservatism of the Estado Novo, came the broad freedoms of the 25th of April revolution. People were thirsty for freedom. It was then that cinemas that only showed porn films appeared, which was a revolution against the taboos of the past and there was a lot of curiosity to see what it was like for some guys to dress up as women.

As there was a lot of interest, there was a lot of money circulating, which allowed the production of pieces of great wardrobe creativity and good professionals dedicated to creating well-structured theatrical pieces.

Over time, there was less interest, there was less money and consequently a greater poverty of means. Artists are not to blame for this. They perform miracles with what they can. The public itself became more superficial and less demanding.

- I have been observing you and I see that you look much younger than your age. Have you had any plastic surgery?

- I did it, and it was worth it. The doctor took 10 years off me. I, for one, wouldn't have done it. I get along very well with aging, which I accept naturally, but Belle Dominique, you know, she was always very vain. She spoke to me, told me she liked to beautify herself on the face and I agreed. We were both satisfied.

- Haven't you done other interventions to make your body more feminine?

- No, never. I have always accepted myself as I am. On stage, thanks to an exquisite wardrobe that cost me a lot and hours of makeup, I was a beautiful woman, but off stage, I never gave up being myself and always maintained my masculine appearance, as you can see.

- It's true, no one would guess that just last week, you wore a dazzling costume with feathers and sequins. That's why they referred to you as the best Portuguese transformist.

- It was the artists themselves who invented this word to distinguish themselves from the transvestites who prostitute themselves on Avenida da Liberdade. In my case, it's true. I never prostituted myself, but several of my colleagues were forced to do so because what they earned from shows was not enough to live on. I, because I had the good sense to always keep a steady job in addition to the shows, didn't go through any needs.

- So, couldn't they do like you, get a job?

- No, it was absolutely impossible for them because they always assumed their female identity. In the way they dress, walk and even talk, in addition to the surgical transformations they underwent. That was silicone for everything, to thicken the lips and cheekbones, the breasts and the butt, until they had a body with feminine shapes. So, no one gave them work, they were ridiculed and even mistreated. The only way to survive was prostitution.

- What drama. I can't even imagine the state of mind with which they approached life.

- Some, very badly. Some suffered from major depression and even committed suicide, poor things.

- Have you personally met any such cases?

- Look, I'm remembering Lydia Barloff, alias, José Manuel Rosado. 40 years ago, he was a great burlesque actor, very successful and to this day he is considered one of the fathers of transformism. He created a caricature of a woman taken to extremes, using exaggerated makeup and gestures.

He participated in Filipe La Féria's show, "Maldita Cocaína" and "Grande Noite".

He participated in several João Baião television programs but he was prone to great depressions and when he felt worst he would take refuge somewhere in the desert, in Morocco, to be alone. He was a hypochondriac and lived in terror of having AIDS, which had already killed many of his friends. When he finally had the courage to take the test, it came back negative. No one understood why he hanged himself when he was 50 and his career was going well.

Domingos Machado's report, punctuated by barely contained emotion, did not fail to touch the journalist. Unconsciously, there was a moment of silence.

- Do you want to tell me about someone else from your time?

- I could talk about several but I'll stick with Ruth Bryden, alias, Joaquim Centúrio de Almeida, who resorted to countless plastic surgeries to become a perfect woman. He felt like a woman and wanted, by all means, to look like a woman. It was a case of publicly admitted transsexualism.

He had belatedly discovered his sexuality in the army, after a quick marriage.

2022

Jornal Expresso. Lisbon

Pedro Freire is a young intern journalist at the newspaper Expresso, who was asked by Laura Sobral to collect data on the murders of minors in Brazil.

- Laura, I already found what you asked me for. There is a lot of information published by the Brazilian press and I tell you that things are scary.

To show you that the problem, a true catastrophe, is not new, see what I found in the archive of the newspaper Folha de São Paulo, from 1987.

Look at these two central pages, which are impressive: 30 small photographs on the left page and another 30 on the right page. These are portraits of the 60 children murdered in the previous month, in the city of São Paulo alone. Below each photograph, a small text summarizes what happened to each of them.

Their ages range from 10 to 18 years old and the stories are very diverse: one of them was shot with a pistol in a small park in the city, in broad daylight, because he was chasing the girlfriend of his supposed friend, who killed   him.

Another 14-year-old boy was killed on demand, with two bullets in the chest, on the street, in broad daylight. The victim had repeatedly robbed an old Portuguese man's store to steal his cash, tobacco and drinks. After several useless complaints made to the police, the old man, in desperation, ordered his death to another 16-year-old boy.

A 13-year-old boy was killed by an older boy, of 15, because he insisted on selling drugs in the same park where he already had his business set up. Four girls, between 12 and 14 years old, turned up dead, showing signs of having been raped.

An 18-year-old boy, openly homosexual, who lived off prostitution, appeared dead in a trash can, showing signs of having been tortured.

A group of 12 boys, between 10 and 14 years old, known to the authorities for being homeless people who robbed tourists every day, in groups of 4 or 5, armed with knives, from whom they extorted money, appeared in the park, all killed at gunpoint shot. The police have already given up on taking them into custody and then having to release them. From time to time, a secret group, known to be made up of police officers, sets up a squad to clean up marginalization in the city, which, at the time, was happening in other large cities, such as Rio de Janeiro.

- My father, continued the young journalist, who in the 80s lived for a while in Rio de Janeiro, told me that at the time, the famous Copacabana beach, had a series of goalposts marking football fields that were open 24 hours a day, with the beach lit up all night, so that the hundreds of homeless children who lived there, escaping the misery of the favelas, could gather in groups that stayed on the beach, day and night. They played ball at night, slept during the day, and only went out, in quick sorties, to rob tourists on Avenida Atlântica.

Despite there being a guardhouse along the 4 kilometers of the Avenue with a police officer post every 300 meters, in the spaces between the guardhouses, a group of 4 to 6 boys, in quick action, surrounded isolated tourists, pointing knives at them and extorting them. They gave them money, with which they go to buy something to eat and return to the beach.

Every now and then, groups of more than a dozen kids shot to death would appear. No one had any doubts that it was the police who killed them in "clearance operations". There were politicians and journalists demanding in the press, the responsibilities, but nothing ever happened to the "death squad".

The Brazilian Public Security Forum – FBSP, published a report entitled "Overview of Lethal and Sexual Violence against Children and Adolescents in Brazil", under the auspices of the United Nations Children's Fund – UNICEF.

The document refers to the existence of more than 7,000 cases of crimes of this nature that occur annually in Brazil, on a scale that makes it impossible for the police to follow all the cases, which have come to be seen as a regrettable statistical banality.

According to the same United Nations document, it reveals that "at least 35,000 children and adolescents were violently killed in Brazil, between 2016 and 2020".

And that "between 2017 and 2020, 180 thousand Brazilian minors suffered sexual violence - an average of 45 thousand per year".

According to the same document, "In 2020, in the 24 Brazilian states for which data is available, a total of 787 deaths of children and adolescents aged 10 to 19 were identified as deaths resulting from police intervention." In the state of São Paulo, in the last five years, 57% of girls killed by police forces between the ages of 15 and 19 were black; among boys the number is even higher: 68%. Up to the age of 14, 77% of victims were black. Statistics like these reflect the notion that the lives of black and poor people have no value in Brazil, says Marisa Fefferman, an activist with the Network for Protection and Resistance Against Genocide and a researcher at the Latin American Council of Social Sciences (CLACSO). "These data demonstrate that the death penalty exists in Brazil and that there is an author who determines who should die and who should live. This has to do with structural racism, it is the logic where there is a suspect subject. The subject who can be killed".

2022

Jornal Expresso. Lisbon

The tireless intern Pedro Freire burst into Laura Sobral's office, announcing to her:

- I have been in contact with ILGA Portugal - Association of Lesbian, Gay, Bisexual, Trans and Intersex Intervention. I spoke with the director and he will give us some contacts of transsexuals who agree to be interviewed. You just have to call him, agreeing the day and time.

From the contacts provided by ILGA, Laura first called an 18 years old young man who agreed to be interviewed in an Expresso meeting room. He was a very tall and incredibly thin young man, with an androgynous appearance. While maintaining his distinctly masculine physiognomy, he wore a short, extravagantly cut, gender neutral hairstyle. He used feminine makeup on his face that left anyone who saw him in doubt as to whether he was a boy with feminine manners or a girl with a boyish appearance. The clothes he was wearing didn't help clarify the doubt. A kind of strapless top partially covered his smooth torso and left his long skeletal arms exposed. There were marks of self-inflicted cuts on his forearms. It was clear that he was a very suffering person who immediately authorized the journalist to mention his name in the article and show his photograph, as he was so committed to denouncing the
atrocities to which a transsexual is subjected in Portugal.

He was accompanied by his mother, who he highlighted as being her great support and who confirmed the pride she had in her son for his courage in accepting his sexual status and reporting the abuse he has been subjected to.

The boy reported that he stopped attending school after successive attacks from classmates and accused school management for not doing anything to punish the aggressors who practice "bullying" indiscriminately and with impunity.

At one point, it was his mother who spoke for him:

- Like any boy of his age, he likes to go out at night, but it's dangerous. I can't force him to stay locked in the house all the time. When he leaves, I stay up all night until he arrives. I never know if my son will come home alive. We all know that young people have been killed outside nightclubs, just because they are different.

A young person is defined as an intersex person who has naturally and equally developed male and female characteristics, which, according to the United Nations, represents 1.7% of the world's population.

- It wasn't my choice. It is a natural condition.

I don't need people to like me. All I need is to be respected and let me live my life in peace, with the right to education, work, fun and the security due to any citizen.

This human story, of a fragile but determined young man, will be the first of a series of interviews that Laura Sobral will carry out, with different types of marginalized and persecuted human beings by society, due to their natural and spontaneous sexual and gender orientation that is not the result of an option but it is only an ineluctable genetic consequence.

2022

ILGA Portugal. Lisbon

Laura, according to the contacts that ILGA provided her, the next interview will be with a young gay man who fled Mauritania and is awaiting a decision from the Portuguese authorities on his request for political asylum.

- Political asylum, why? For what purpose? - Laura wondered.

On the day and time agreed between the management of ILGA Portugal and Pedro Freire, Laura Sobral presented herself at the headquarters of the LGBTI+ organization (the updated name of LBGT), on Rua dos Fanqueiros. The young man was accompanied by the organization's lawyer, defending his case with the Portuguese authorities, who identified herself as Dr. Pamela, whose surname she did not mention, not wanting to see it published in the press.

Young Omar Al-Rashidi, a 20-year-old Arab, well dressed and educated, claiming to be the son of a wealthy family, introduced himself in perfect French that he had learned at the Lycée Français Théodore Mouad, in Nouakchott, capital of the Islamic Republic of Mauritania, where, despite the official language being Arabic, several dialects and languages survive, in the tradition of a former French colony, wealthy families continue to send their children to study at the Lycée Français.

The father holds a high administrative position as director of the port that had been modernized by the Chinese into a deep-water port, which allows it to receive large ships, of great importance for the entire Saharan Atlantic coast.

- How did you end up here? – Laura asked. Why Portugal and not France, with which your country will certainly have more relations?

- I am aware that France is making it as difficult as possible to accept more refugees, as it cannot even control the thousands who have been concentrated in the Calais area for years, trying unsuccessfully to enter the United Kingdom, in addition to the many which are already spread throughout France.

Even in Paris, there are avenues completely transfigured by the presence of hundreds of camping tents.

Emmanuel Macron's government is negotiating with the government of Rwanda to finance the creation of refugee camps to send all those who are illegally in France, regardless of which country they are from, just as the European Union is doing with Turkey, paying to receive the 3.7 million Syrian refugees already there.

I knew that Portugal, being less sought after by refugees than other countries in central Europe, has maintained a more humane policy regarding this issue.

- And how did you travel here?

- There are organizations that are exploring the very profitable business of bringing refugees to Europe and simultaneously carrying out drug trafficking.

The closest destination is the Canary Islands, but as this route is already well known to the Spanish authorities, it is no longer used because fast navy ships of the Spanish navy are there, waiting for the traffickers.

Therefore, the current solution is to disembark at night on a deserted beach in the Algarve coast, after an endless journey in the cold and hunger, and vomiting the soul, in the company of Guineans, Malians and Senegalese.

- So why did you want to leave the country? You must have had a privileged life there, right? - Asked the journalist.

- In fact, I am not, nor do I intend to be, an economic refugee. I think I can be equated with a political refugee.

- Why? Are you part of the opposition to the government? Do you have sympathy for the Polisario Front or Al-Quaeda?

- Nothing like that. Just because I'm gay.

- So, what does this have to do with the fact that you requested Political Asylum?

- According to the Mauritanian legislation, subordinated to Sharia, or Islamic Law, all LGBTI+ activities are considered illegal and homosexuality is subject to the penalty of stoning to death in public.

- Let me interrupt your dialogue, but I must clarify that there is a misunderstanding here - the lawyer, Dr. Pamela, intervened.

- The asylum request does not necessarily have to be made due to political reasons, which in this case do not even exist. According to the 1951 Geneva Convention relating to the Status of Refugees, anyone subject to persecution in their country has the right to request international protection. Article 19 of the Charter of Fundamental Rights of the European Union prohibits the extradition of anyone who is at risk of being subjected to the death penalty, torture or other mistreatment, or inhuman or degrading punishment.

The Common European Asylum System - SECA, establishes the conditions for being considered a refugee or beneficiary of protection that confers a set of rights such as residence permit, travel documents, access to employment, social security and healthcare. Now, personally, I believe that Mr. Omar meets these conditions and does not need any financial support from the Portuguese State, because he benefits from family support to pay his necessary expenses.

- And when do you expect to see your right to asylum recognized? - Asked the journalist.

- I don't know. I'm still waiting for a resolution.

- What is happening - said Dr. Pamela, is that, as I was informed, there are jurists on the committee that decides these cases, who are in doubt and think that the asylum request may not be justified, due to the fact that in practice, it appears that in Mauritania, although such a law exists, in reality, the penalty for stoning to death has never been applied. But we argue that the fact is not relevant, since the existence of the law, having not been revoked, one never knows when a more orthodox Islamic leader decides to put it into practice. Isn't it true that Al-Quaeda seeks to impose itself in Mauritania? Then? All they have to do is take power and Sharia will be fulfilled.

2022

Expresso newspaper

The management of ILGA Portugal suggested to Laura Sobral, as the journalist was writing about the persecution of the LGBTI+ community, that it would be important to interview the German Manfred Lashek, from the management of ILGA Germany, who would have a lot to inform about the calamity taking place in Chechnya. He asked if she was interested.

- Yes, of course I'm interested.

- In that case, I'll ask him if he wants to do the interview via video conference.

- Manfred will be at your disposal via Skype, tomorrow at 3:00 pm, Lisbon time.

- Thank you very much. You can confirm with him that it is booked.

- Very good. His name on Skype is this – and he handed her a piece of paper with his contact information.

- Good afternoon, Manfred. Thank you very much for your availability. I'm Laura Sobral, a journalist for Expresso newspaper and I'm writing a series of articles to denounce certain realities unknown to the general public, about the LGBTI+ community. I am informed that you have great knowledge of what is happening in Chechnya.

- Laura, nice to meet you. I can tell you a lot about what is happening there but I start by recommending that you try to see the film "Welcome to Chechnya", by director David France (2020) about the activities of a group of activists of which I am part, in defense of LGBTI+ threatened by the country's regime.

- What's happening must have something to do with the state religion, right?

- Certainly. The majority of Chechens are Sunni Muslims, where the influence of more orthodox Islam is felt and what is happening there is not very different from what is happening in other Muslim countries, in the 21st century, however much of it may surprise us.

For example, since 2019, the sultan of Borneo, Hassanal Bolkiah, who holds the position of supreme leader of Islam in the country, instituted Islamic Sharia law, and began to apply the death penalty by stoning for crimes of homosexuality or of adultery, and the mutilation of the foot or hand, due to theft, also the death penalty for blasphemy, defamation of the name of the prophet Muhammad, or for apostasy; and flogging for abortion, among other archaic penalties.

- Really, it's unbelievable - reacted the journalist.

- The same Sharia law, with public execution, is provided for in the Constitution of many Islamic countries such as Saudi Arabia, Somalia, Sudan, Iran.

Public execution was widely practiced by Daesh, during the period in which the Islamic State dominated part of Syria and Iraq.

Law enforcement varies greatly from country to country. There are some that express a certain tolerance, such as Mauritania, Egypt, Tunisia, Indonesia, Lebanon, Kosovo, Bosnia, Albania and the United Arab Emirates, although homosexuals in these countries do not risk to express themselves, living their lives in the greatest secret.

However, and surprisingly, some inconsistencies are known, especially in Afghanistan.

The same Taliban, who apply a brutal interpretation of Sharia, which prohibits women from going out on the streets unless in the company of a man, are forced to wear the burqa and can no longer attend school, compared to men, they allow themselves some certain freedoms that are traditional among the Pashtun, the predominant ethnic group among the Taliban. Although Sharia imposes the death penalty and honor killing carried out by the family of homosexuals, sexual pleasure between men is a relatively common practice among Islamic radicals. According to their interpretation, as they are married and have children, they cannot be considered homosexuals.

This occurs as a consequence of their cultural tradition, according to which women are considered only as bearers of children. In most Afghan couples, there is no affinity between husband and wife, as a result of marriages being arranged by families when they were still children. Many couples only meet on their wedding day. It is therefore more natural that affinity may occur between men. During the wars that have been fought, many families sent their sons to boarding schools in Pakistan, where they were raped by teachers. Hence, tradition has accustomed them to considering the situation as normal.

In Afghanistan, it is common practice to kidnap boys to be raped by adults. This practice of relationships between adult men and boys and adolescents, known as *bacha bazi* (playing with boys) was banned between 1996 and 2001, during the Afghan Civil War, and became subject to Sharia law, as for any homosexual, but it was not applied to powerful offenders, due to the conniving attitude of the police.

There are reports from 2007 that confirm the continuation of the practice of *bacha bazi* in Northern Afghanistan. The boys are dressed in women's clothing and forced to participate in dances and sexual acts.

- That tells us a lot. We had no idea.

- In many countries, including Chechnya, - continued Manfred - which is part of the Russian Federation, honor killings of homosexuals by their families are promoted. In Chechnya, it is the President Ramzan Kadyrov himself who asks their families to kill them.

Since 2017, the State has promoted a series of purges against the LGBTI+ community. Around 100 gay men were taken prisoners in concentration camps, where they were subjected to torture, some disappeared forever, and three of them were murdered.

A journalist, revealing official sources who defined the case as a "prophylactic sweep", reported the event, but had to go into hiding.

- But what has your group done to protect the victims from official persecution?

- In complete secrecy, we have managed to evacuate 4 to 8 people from Chechnya at a time to our organization's safe houses in Moscow and Leningrad, from where they cannot leave, sometimes for months, waiting for us to obtain forged documents for them to leave Russia, and to have guarantees of reception in other countries that give them initial support to start a life as refugees who will never be able to return to their country. While they are confined there, there is always someone from our group who brings them the groceries so they can cook, and who pays the electricity, water and gas bills.

- And who pays for all this?

- We receive generous regular support from several LGBTI+ organizations from different countries.

- And have you already brought many people from there?

- Almost a hundred, but there are many more to come.

- Thank you very much, Manfred, for your valuable clarification on a situation that is unknown here in Portugal. I will try to publish the information in my newspaper. Good luck in continuing your work.

Pedro Freire, who had attended the video conference, remembered to add a piece of information he had found during his Google searches:

- You might be interested in mentioning in your article about this issue of Chechnya something that happened in 2017 in our National Assembly, which has since been forgotten by the public. At the time, the Left Bloc presented to the Assembly a proposal to condemn the government of Chechnya, which is semi-autonomous from the Russian Federation, with its own laws, for the official homophobic persecution of the LGBTI+ population by the State. The proposal was approved with favorable votes from all benches, except the PCP, Portuguese Communist Party, which abstained.

- It is not surprising. They had already supported the invasion of Hungary and Czechoslovakia, during the Soviet Union. They lamented the fall of the Berlin Wall and the fall of the Soviet Union. Now, they have even approved the invasion of Ukraine by the Russian Federation. All for Mother Russia.

- In my opinion, they are shooting themselves in the foot. Every time there are elections, they lose more deputies. They once had 31 and now they only have 6. If they continue like this, next time they might even lose their seats in Parliament.

2022

Avenida de Roma

During the interview at ILGA headquarters, with the young man from Mauritania, Laura Sobral was curious to meet Dr. Pamela, the Brazilian citizen who had surprised her by not wanting to reveal her surname.

At ILGA, they know little about her, only that she provides pro bono, as a lawyer, support services to members of the LGBTI+ community helps the Association with *pro bono* legal support.

It is obvious that she is a young lady, just over 30 years old, beautiful, openly transsexual, very elegant, who could have been a catwalk model, dresses impeccably, with exquisite good taste, not at all exhibitionist and reveals that she benefits from a high standard of life.

It is only known that she is a premature widow and lives in a mansion in Serra de Sintra, a family heirloom.

Laura had asked her assistant to contact her, requesting an interview. She refused, delicately, because she wants to maintain the privacy of her personal life - informed Pedro Freire.

- We may not even mention the name or give him a pseudonym.

- Even so. I told her about this possibility but she doesn't want to expose her life.

Pedro Freire, always eager to provide his boss with the necessary assistance, has found it very difficult to give her the contact she wants.

- Laura, you asked me to look for a Brazilian transvestite advertised on various prostitution websites, who would agree to be interviewed. I've made more than 20 phone calls and every one of them, as soon as I mention that it's for an interview with a newspaper, they hang up the phone, without even saying anything.

- It's natural. Keep trying. Use your charm. Tell her the interview is with a female journalist, not you. Maybe it makes a difference. It's a woman-to-woman conversation.

- I have made 12 more calls. Finally, I found one who agreed to be interviewed and said it could even bring publicity to her business. On the website, she says she is a porn star and provides several links to her films. I went to see them and it is confirmed that it is the same one that appears in the ad on the viptransex.net website. She has worked in several European countries and considers herself a top luxury escort. But she only agrees to give the interview if the newspaper pays her 500 Euros for an hour of conversation.

- Do you have photographs of her?

- You can see her here at viptransex.net.

- Really, she is a women's show. Tall, very elegant, a perfect body, a beautiful black face. No one would say she is a man.

- Go through the photographs. Take a good look at the latest.

- What! I had no idea there was material like this!

- Then? Back there, in the text, it says it is 24 centimeters. It's a measure of a large black person.

- I'm going to talk to the boss – concluded Laura.

Laura went to discuss the matter with her editor in chief, as there was no provision for payment to such interviews.

After learning about the matter and seeing the photographs, which made his eyes widen, Artur Varela picked up the phone and called the financial director:

- João, Laura needs 500 bucks to go to whores.

The interview was scheduled for Adriana residence, advertised as being a luxury apartment, with all amenities and privacy, somewhere in Avenida de Roma. She informed the door number, but didn't say the floor.

- When you get to the door, call me again so I can tell you the floor. On the 5th Right, a door opened, with no one in sight. From behind the door, a voice was heard:

- Come in, come in.

In the dimly lit entrance hall, Larissa was waiting, in exquisite lingerie, with very good taste, as Laura could see.

- If it's not Victoria's Secret, at its best, it's looks like it, thought Laura, knowledgeable on the subject.

- Hi, honey, make yourself comfortable. Come with me.

Initially nervous about the situation, Laura felt more at ease when she realized she had been taken to a room, not a bedroom.

With an affable smile and a lot of sympathy in her voice, the hostess explained:

- My dear. As used in the profession, you must pay first.

- Yes, of course, that's fine. And she handed her an envelope. She was surprised that it hadn't been opened, an unexpected sign of delicacy.

The first visual impression was enlightening to the fact that perhaps 10 years must have passed since the photographs she had seen. The same beauty, the same elegance and a posture with a certain finesse were present but the face, although impeccably made up, already showed some intervention of time.

- If I were a consumer, I would say that the website's advertising is misleading, thought Laura.

- Shall we start? Do you mind if I turn on this recorder?

- No problem, my dear.

- You could start by saying where you are from, what your childhood and youth were like, when you felt you were in the wrong body.

- I'm from Alagoinhas, near Salvador da Bahia, in the Brazilian Northeast.

I was born in a poor family, the youngest of three brothers.

Since I was a child, I preferred to play with dolls with the neighboring girls, instead of playing boyish games with my brothers. Being the Benjamin of the family, I was pampered and protected by everyone and they didn't give any importance to the case.

It was only when I started school that I started to have problems because I didn't fit in with the other kids. They started attacking me until my brothers noticed and beat my attackers to the ground. Since then, no one has messed with me again, even though they looked at me with contempt.

I think I spent a childhood without any major doubts about my identity that disturbed me. However, as I entered puberty, I started to feel like something was wrong with my body. I had a dick but I felt like a girl, but I was embarrassed to confess this to anyone, not even my brothers, who I loved very much and protected me.

I made an effort not to express this tendency of mine, until I was 16, the age at which any Brazilian boy has already had at least one girlfriend or is already doing odd jobs to have money for whores. One day, my father didn't beat around the bush when he asked me:

- Look, don't you like women? Are you homosexual?

I made the biggest mistake of my life when, naively, I decided to answer him honestly:

- I don't feel like a guy. I feel like a girl.

- What?

I received a massive beating that left me in bed for three days, with bruises all over my body.

My father waited for me to get out of bed to tell me:

- Put yourself on the street and never come back, because you are the shame of the family. You disgust me.

My mother gave me some money and I took the bus to Salvador. There are many tourists there who are looking for cheap sex. If I didn't want to starve, I had to accept that. I joined others who sold their bodies for little more than a plate of food.

- What was the prostitution environment like in Salvador?

- Very bad, very bad, really. Too much, a real jungle. Therefore, everyone tries to get money to get out of there, preferably, flee to Europe, but few succeed.

The competition on the street was very big. Above all, it was girls who were most sought after. Trans people, like me, wanted to earn money to transform their bodies and become more in demand. We were subjected to all kinds of violence and abuse, by society in general, by passersby, by the police, by our own family and by some clients who behave like wild animals. And also, by colleagues on the same street, where hierarchies are established, either by seniority, or by violence, in the allocation of the best places on the street and the best times, even the obligation to pay protection to the street boss, an older pimp, who imposes the operating rules in the area of his or her hierarchical domain. We lived in terror of being taken to prison, to be raped by the guards. Some became desperate and mutilated themselves. It was always safer to be transferred to a hospital than to remain in a prison cell.

- What about pimps? Didn't they have pimps?

- Prostitutes do. They are exploited, all the money they earn is for them, but they benefit from their protection. It's slavery.

With trans sisters, it's different. They have the pimp, who they pay for the place on the street, just like a place rental, but they don't pay for what they earn from customers. Some have husbands, for personal protection.

- In this case, the husband is the pimp, right?

- It's not quite the same thing. Although none of them work, the person who manages the money is generally the trans woman, who feeds and clothes the husband, but wants to be able to get rid of him and replace him with somebody else, although sometimes this causes scenes of violence and even death. In Brazil, it's better not to have a husband. I didn't have one.

- When did you start to transform your body?

- As soon as I could. A year after arriving in Salvador, I started hormonal treatment and, little by little, as I earned money, I started pumping. I was lucky, I did it well, but for some sisters, things went very wrong and they were deformed.

- How long did it take to reach your current appearance?

- After just over two years, I was ready and started earning real money, but I also spent it because my father was sick and sent money home, saying I worked as a waiter in a restaurant in Rio.

- I learned that some trans people, no matter how feminine they become, are never satisfied and continue, throughout their lives, to add another touch here, another touch there. Is this your case?

- No. I'm satisfied with the result and I'm not paranoid about adding silicone here and there. I understand the sisters who do this, all of us, we want to be more beautiful, more than real women. I don't feel that need. It may be that when I'm older, I'll have to fix something, but I won't want major interventions.

- When did you come to Portugal? How was your arrival? Was it one of those who traffic people for prostitution who brought you?

- No. At least, for Portugal, I don't know what it's like for the rest of Europe, it's not some mafia organization that brings us, as happens with women, into prostitution, who are locked up for months or years in an alterna bar, from where they can't leave. Their passport is taken away from them and they do not receive the money they earn from clients, until they pay for the plane ticket, accommodation and food and where they are kept, without knowing when slavery ends.

I don't know anyone in this field, but it is said that some are fed with drugs, which never releases them from the "contract", until they are decrepit and sold to other lower-level traffickers. I don't know if this still happens, but I heard that it has already happened in some pass houses spread across the country, however, closed by the police, where they found, in the majority, girls from the East who had tricked themselves into working contracts that didn't exist.

In the trans community, things work differently.

There's always one that came first. She came to explore the environment, made money and proved that it is much safer to be in Portugal. Then, she pays for a friend's ticket and settles in her house, where they work together. This is seen as a great help, so the sister who orders others to come is known as mother, or godmother.

Naturally, the money advanced is to be paid with interest, at a previously agreed percentage, as the new arrival works, and the clearly inflated expenses of the woman's income of the house rent, water, electricity, gas, TV channels and Internet must be paid for all, normally two or three in the same house, in addition to paying the godmother, half of what they receive from each client. Cable television is mandatory in every home to watch Brazilian channels and a Wi Fi connection to the Internet is essential for advertising the services and communicating on social media. Each one has their own cell phone, which is essential for serving customers.

So, all rules are well established, from the outset, everyone is committed to charging the same to customers, so that unfair price competition is not established in the same house and, to know, from the outset, the exact amount that each one must pay immediately to the godmother.

- Do you mean to say that houses are simultaneously a place of work and a home?

- Yes of course.

- It seems like your business, being you a godmother.

- Of course, it is. That's why many of us, after paying our debts to our godmother, want to be godmothers too. We started making money, we bring others and the business started to pay off. But be careful, we also have expenses. The rental contract is not made in our name. The house is rented to a Portuguese person or a Brazilian who is legal, who sublets it, always for a value well above market prices. The way to make the house cheaper is to marry a Portuguese person and the rent is made in his name.

- We know that many Brazilian trans women travel through various cities in Europe and that, when they are in Portugal, they are either in Lisbon, or at other times in Porto, or in Coimbra, or in Faro, or in any other city. Why so much turnover?

- It is a necessity of the profession. Although, in each city, we have a few regular customers, they alone are not enough to make real money. New customers are needed every day. It is a clientele that is always looking for some new trans. Only a few remain regular customers. Therefore, it is necessary to always be rotating. The system of sharing houses with other sisters allows this rotation. We can stay a week, or two, or a month, in Lisbon and then go on a "tour" to other cities, or to other countries, always looking for new clients. Traveling by road, it is possible to cross Europe in the Schengen Area, without being asked for documentation. We are undocumented in Europe, just as we are here, where, in compliance with the law, we can only stay as a tourist for three months and then another three months if we prove that we have the means to subsist for that period. But in reality, due to lack of inspection by the authorities, there are those who have been here for 15 years or more, without documents. The safest thing, whether to work here or in other cities in Europe, the best, is to marry a European citizen. That's what I did. I married a Portuguese man. I was given a residence permit, which allows me to rent a house in my name, known as a European Union Citizen Family Card.

- Do you live with your husband?

- No. I paid him for the wedding, now that same sex marriage is recognized in Portugal. I sent him away straight away. There was no affinity between us.

- This means that on your identity document you are still a man, right?

- Yeah. I still haven't been able to request a change of gender and name, which is also possible here in Portugal. It's not important to me. I know who I am and what I am and I don't need to prove anything to anyone.

- How is your current relationship with your family?

- It has changed a lot since I started sending money for treatments for my father, who suffered from cancer, which, fortunately, he recovered from. Today, he knows who I am because I went to visit him, as a woman. He was shocked. But he struggled to understand. The proximity of death transformed him greatly and made him more tolerant and understanding. My mother and brothers adore me. They think I was very brave in coming out and they are even proud of me. I'm at peace with the family.

- Are you thinking about having surgery to remove your penis and create a vagina?

- No way! How horrible! I have a horror of surgeries and then, how could I live without my greatest attribute, which is my livelihood? And it also gives me a lot of pleasure. Don't you want to try it? Since you paid, you are entitled to the full service.

- No, thank you. That's not what I came for.

- You don't even know what you're missing, my dear.

- But I imagine. Thank you very much for your precious collaboration.

2022

Expresso newspaper

During the coffee break, at the newspaper's headquarters, the editor in chief, Artur Varela, Laura Sobral and assistant Pedro Freire, gathered.

- Laura, said the assistant: I was listening to the recording you made in the interview with the transvestite Adriana and some of her statements aroused my curiosity to research the subject. For example, she fled Brazil to escape the wave of murders that occur there every year. Take a look at what I found out about the subject:

Number of transsexuals murdered between 2008 and 2021: 1,645.

Number of transgender people murdered between 2017 and 2021:2017

- 1792018

- 1632019

- 1242020

- 1752021

- 140

Last year, 96.4% of the victims were trans women, which is not surprising, because the number of trans men, I know, is much lower, but I don't know by how much.

81% were 35 years old at most.

81% were black, which leaves no doubt about the racist nature, combined with the homophobic one.

78% were sex workers.

7.5% of the homicides took place in public spaces. Killing people in the middle of the street, in full view of passersby, is common in Brazil.

- How horrible! Laura said. It's really easy to understand why they flee, especially to here, and it's also because of the language. And because, as she said, the security here has nothing to do with the barbarity in Brazil.

- Of course, you can't compare the security, or rather, the insecurity in Portugal and Brazil – intervened Artur, who, being the oldest, had memories of earlier occurrences.

Laura must remember, but Pedro was still a child when that murder of a homeless transvestite occurred in Porto, do you remember, Laura?

- Yes, it was an horrific story, the case that went around the world, of poor Gilberta, barbarically murdered by 14 boys, between the ages of 12 and 16.

- It was precisely because I remembered a case that happened last year, that of the transsexual Angelita, whose body was found in an advanced state of decomposition on Matosinhos Beach – interrupted Pedro, which aroused my curiosity to know if there had been other previous cases. And I discovered a lot of information about this case of Gilberta and another one, Luna, another transsexual who was a prostitute in Lisbon, in the Conde Redondo area. I took notes on these three cases, for Laura to use, if she sees any interest in them.

- You see, Artur? The boy is full of initiative. Maybe it's time to finish his internship and start writing his own articles. What do you think?

- I can see that he is. The boy has potential. He has a future.

- I have no problem with him writing an article on the subject, which is justified and should be interspersed between mine.

- Very good. Pedro, start typing an article about the murder of transvestites in Portugal, so that the subject is not forgotten.

2022

Expresso newspaper

Young Pedro Freire proudly reviewed his first article published in the issue of Expresso, which he had waited anxiously for, at the printer's mouth, already in his hand, which represented his official debut as an investigative journalist.

Having been suggested to write about the crimes committed in Portugal against transsexuals, he discovered only three past cases that had been published in the press. One of them might not even have been a crime.

Having carried out an exhaustive search, he was surprised not to find more cases, what spoke well of the great difference in tolerance between Portugal and Brazil.

The most logical thing to do would be to report the three in chronological order but, considering the fact that the severity of each one has been decreasing over time, he concluded that the most serious crime should be reserved for the end of the article, the one with the greatest impact, a monstrous apotheosis.

- I don't know if I'll be accused of sensationalism, but the best thing to do, according to the rules, is to wait always until the end – that's what he thought.

He started with the most recent case, from 2021, in fact, the least traumatic for sensitive readers, that one of a young woman whose body was found in an advanced state of decomposition in Matosinhos beach, Angelita Seixas Alves Correia, a 31years old transsexual, born in Goiânia, Brazil, worked in Portugal

as a personal trainer and dance instructor.

She had moved to Portugal in 2016, to the city of Matosinhos, where she got married in 2018.

On January 1st, she left home, having informed her husband that she was going to a friend's house. After that, she was never seen alive again. Meanwhile, Angelita had confided to her sister that she was scared because she had been receiving death threats from strangers via Telegram on her cell phone.

Angelita's body was found by a surfer, who called the police. Some of his personal items were found in his clothes.

The expertise carried out by the police indicated that there was no evidence of a third-party intervention in her death, which was due to drowning, and the idea of murder was discarded, but the doubt persists to this day because Angelita left a video on Facebook in which she complained of being persecuted and the victim of threats.

Whether it was a crime or not remains unknown to this day.

The Conde Redondo area in Lisbon, although it is a residential and commercial neighborhood, at night turns into a "red light" neighborhood, with dozens of sex workers roaming the street, offering their services. Women, men and transsexuals competing for the best places at traffic lights, when the red light turns on and drivers are forced to stop.

Luna, a 43-year-old transsexual, old in the neighborhood, and still with notable success, already had a permanent place on the corner of Conde Redondo and Ferreira Lapa street. She was in the last phase of psychotherapy consultations at a hospital in Lisbon, which precede sexual reassignment surgery. She intended to become an "operated", without a penis and with the construction of a neovagina, to fulfill her desire to be a woman. Whether she would have more or less demand later, she would soon see.

Since February 19th, 2008, Luna was no longer seen, neither in the street nor in the room of the boarding house where she lived and worked, for four years.

Days passed without any news from her. The boarding house vacated the room and stored his belongings. In the area, it was thought that she had been arrested.

It didn't occur to anyone to notify the police of her disappearance.

On February 28th, an employee of a company that removed industrial and construction waste, discovered the body of a woman, in an advanced state of decomposition. It would have ended up there, after being deposited in a city trash container that traveled to Loures in a truck from a solid waste transport company.

Naturally, the case interested the Pink Panther Association, the Front to Combat Homophobia, which decided to investigate. Its president, Sérgio Vitorino, who had been working for a long time with Conde Redondo's prostitutes, declared that he had found no evidence of organized crime and concluded that it would be another "hate crime", judging by the marks on the neck and the results of the autopsy. It was known that she was the victim of constant extortion attempts.

The perpetrator of the crime was never found.

Born in São Paulo, an urban jungle with 12 million inhabitants, Gilberto, at the age of 14, told his mother that he was "going to be a woman", only after his father died without ever knowing that his son was like that. In front of his family, he wore more or less neutral clothes, but it was at his friends' houses that he dressed as a woman. Due to the news of discrimination and deaths of homosexuals that occurred in São Paulo, not wanting to end up like them, he decided to flee to France, when he was 18 years   old. He returned to Brazil, where he underwent hormone therapy, silicone implantation and minor facial correction surgeries.

He returned to France, where he spent two years, now with a woman's body, and later went to Portugal, where he lived for the remaining twenty years of his life.

He settled in Porto, where he started attending gay nights, with great success as a flamboyant blonde, who had no shortage of customers. At Kilt, one of the first gay bars in Porto, the new Gilberta started doing transformism shows, as a joke, and then moved on to the bars Bustos and Syndicato, playing the diva Marilyn Monroe in the song "Diamants are the girl's best friend".

During the day, she walked with her two Yorkshire Terrier puppies, the company that made her happy.

One day, she left the front door open and the dogs ran out into the street. They died after being run over, much to the dismay of Gilberta, who fell into depression and became more isolated from contact with her friends.

Over the years, its freshness was lost, its voluptuous shapes could not resist the effects of gravity, age and weight gain. Progressively, she lost clients over the years, until she reached a level of poverty that took her to the canteen for the poor, at the "O Coração da Cidade" Association, where she had lunch and dinner, where she was known for her politeness and friendliness.

As she no longer had money to pay for a room, she looked for a dilapidated building, where she improvised a tent with materials collected from the trash, where she remained the entire time.

At the age of 45, too old for her profession, sick and suffering from AIDS, increasingly weakened, she began to lead a homeless life, an hermit, in the old abandoned building, where she only left to go to the charity meals.

One day, three boys who were playing there discovered her, spoke to her, created a good relationship and even brought her rice which they cooked for her.

The relationship with the boys changed radically when they informed other colleagues at Oficinas de São José, an institution to promote the protection of young people at risk, that they had met a man "with breasts". Soon the others appeared, a total of 14, curious to know about this abnormality. They started by demanding him to show them the sex, to make sure if it was a man or a woman. When they verified that he was a man, they decided that what they should do was to beat the abnormal man to the ground. Unable to defend herself, Gilberta was robbed by the gang, with kicks, punches and beatings, which left her inert. They returned in the following days for the fun of the day, in which everyone participated, which was "beating up Gi". For seven consecutive days, the ritual was repeated, until on February 21th, 2006, when they noticed that she no longer moved, even when they touched her wounds, they concluded that she was dead.

Then the question arose of deciding what to do with the body. Their first thought was to bury her in the middle of the building's ruins, but they gave up on the idea because they didn't have a shovel.

They then thought about burning him but gave up the idea when one of them drew attention to the danger of the smoke alerting passersby in the region.

They then decided to wrap the victim's body in a blanket, which was dragged 100 meters to a well, where it was thrown. As the well had plenty of water, the body sank and was no longer visible.

One of the boys wanted to boast about his achievement and reported the incident to others. The news spread like a wildfire and reached the police, which went to remove the body.

The Attorney General's Office took the 14 defendants to trial in the Criminal Courts. In the first phase, Victor Santos, the oldest of the group, being 16 years old, was already imputable and has been subject to a heavy sentence for qualified homicide. What saved him was the testimony of the other 13, who claimed that he never attacked Gilberta, and simply watched. He was sentenced to eight months in prison for the crime of failing to help the victim.

In the first phase of the process, the other 13 minors were held responsible for "co-authoring a crime of qualified homicide, in the attempted form and as possible intent".

However, the autopsy confirmed that the cause of death was drowning and not assault, concluding that the victim had been thrown into the well, still alive, although unconscious.

Eleven of the remaining 13 defendants, accused of committing a crime of qualified bodily harm, were sentenced to imprisonment for between eleven and thirteen months in an Educational Center and the remaining two, accused only of the crime of omission of assistance to the victim, the guardianship monitoring measure was applied in an educational institution.

The case, which raised a huge stir at the time and provoked a debate about transsexuality, was widely publicized by the national and foreign press and had unexpected repercussions.

The sexual abuse suffered by boys at Oficinas de São José, an institution dependent on the Catholic Church, which took in children from dysfunctional homes, children of alcoholic or chemically dependent parents or prostitutes, which led to the director's suicide, during the the trial, and the institution has been closed.

2022

Expresso newspaper

Laura Sobral met Pedro Freire to decide new themes for the series of articles on LGBTI+.

- I'm in doubt about what other people to interview, whose human stories are interesting to the general public and help greater acceptance of the gay community, said Laura, to begin with.

- Don't call a transgender person, gay or she'll get offended. Deep down, she feels like a woman, so having sex with men is what is normal and expected of a woman.

- You are right. I have to be careful with that.

- You could interview someone very well known. There is no shortage of actors, singers, dancers, models, politicians, painters, writers, television presenters, who everybody knows and have already come out publicly.

- Yes, some have even given interviews. Not long ago we heard Catarina Deslandes confess that she feels equally attracted to men and women and, curiously, if she was the target of several criticisms, it wasn't even because of that. It was because she showed her butt, or because she gained weight and slovenly in appearance.

- It's curious that no one criticizes an actor like Diogo Infante, or TV figures like Manuel Luís Goucha, Cláudio Ramos, or José Carlos Malato, why is that?

- Because they are respected and respectful people. They lead a normal life, without displaying their sexual condition. They preserve their privacy but, if they are asked to talk about the subject, they either do so openly, because they have nothing to hide, or they prefer not to come out publicly. They give each other respect.

- Look, there are even those who decide to come out publicly, before the press discovers their sexual orientation and starts creating a wave of gossip about their life. That's what Paulo Rangel did, very intelligently, when he ran for leadership of the PSD, Social Democrat Party. Before anyone would reveal that he is gay, something that was not of public knowledge, he took action and shut down the gossip before they got out. Conclusion: he won points, personally and politically and no one bothered him.

- I get the impression that there are people who, surprisingly, even seem to gain greater popularity, precisely because they are gay. Does anyone care about the fact that António Variações was openly gay? Or the poet Ary dos Santos? Or painters, like Mário Cesariny or Maluda? Or the big international names in music, like Liberace, Prince, Ney Mato Grosso, David Bowie, Freddy Mercury, Boy George, Elton John? No. What remained for the future was his art.

- But some are true aberrations. Remember that Conchita Wurst, the Austrian who won the Eurovision contest in 2014? Dressed as a woman, down to the feet, and displaying long black hair, a mustache and a bushy beard?
After winning the competition, he became a highly respected figure and was invited to sing at Galas at the European Parliament, at the United Nations offices in Vienna, and at Sydney Opera House.

- She may sing very well, but she's a Drag Queen that disgusts me. Dressed as a woman and with a beard? There's another one that disgusts me, but it's because of his personality, a disgusting person.

- Who?

- José Castelo Branco.

- There are already two of us. It's not because he's gay, it's because he has a personality that's disgusting.

- Good. Forward. Do you know anything about trans beauty pageants? I've vaguely heard about that, asked Laura.

- Yes, I've already been researching this. It's not clear why, but there are two international competitions and I was looking at the final year candidates. Miss Trans Star International 2022 has already taken place. Do you want to see the final here? It is worth it. Opened a video on You Tube.

- Yeah man, is this more than three hours long? Don't even think I'm going to see that.

- No problem. I drag this to the end so you can see just who the two finalists were: Miss Nicaragua and Miss Mexico.Look, Miss Nicaragua won. For me, I would give the crown to Miss Mexico. She is much more feminine and much prettier. It's more of a sexy style, while the other is taller and has a catwalk mannequin style body. No one would say they were once men.

- Or do they continue to be?

- I don't know. I didn't look for the Application Regulations. I don't know if they are "operated" or not.

- You said you have another contest- There is Miss Trans Global, which last year was won by Miss India. This year, they are still collecting applications. But I was looking at last year's pageant and it is of much lower quality than Miss Trans Star International.

This one seems a bit third world. There are few beautiful candidates, the majority have masculine features, others are pot-bellied, others have fat legs, far from what is required in a female beauty contest.

- Do you know if any Portuguese woman has already participated?

- In 2016, Portuguese Sarah Inês Moreira, 29 years old, from Porto, participated in the fourth edition of Miss Trans Star International competition, which took place in Barcelona, but was poorly classified. For me, she was a bit macho.

- I have a vague idea that a few years ago, I heard a transsexual competing for Miss Universe. Do you know anything about this?

- Google knows everything. Look, here: Spanish transgender Ângela Ponce won Miss Spain and applied for Miss Universe 2018. This happens because in 2012, the organization lifted the ban on transgender candidates and the jury started to be made up only of women.

Angela, 26, from Andalusia, had previously been rejected from other beauty contests. She volunteers at a Spanish non-profit organization that works with families and children who deal with problems linked to gender identity, children who suffer discrimination for being different and even think   about   suicide. She considers that she was very lucky because she has always had the greatest support from her parents, which was of great importance for the formation of her personality, which made her a tireless fighter for LGBTI+ rights.

- I don't know if you understand this issue of public figures sexuality. It's difficult for me to understand why, if a gay person is a public figure, he can even be liked and if he is a nobody, he is most likely to be the target of homophobia.

- Maybe you have to interview a sociologist, or a psychologist, who can enlighten you.

- And you, do you have any projects?

- I have. I'll ask Artur if he is interested. I'm thinking about taking a week off to visit my brother in Switzerland and take the opportunity to interview Roberta Close.

- What do you think?

- That will be interesting.

SWITZERLAND

2022

Swiss Alps

It wasn't difficult for Pedro Freire to find out Roberta Close's address. When searching her name on Google, the Brazilian transsexual who became known all over the world, has no less than 52,400,000 references!

Practically all of them mention that she lives in Zurich, Switzerland and is married to Roland Granacher, a senior manager at Nestlé.

They are two public figures, well-known in Swiss high society, frequenters of social, cultural and charitable events, often covered in the pink press.

The phone number that Pedro got was that of her husband, who answered him sympathetically, when he identified himself as a journalist from the Portuguese newspaper Expresso.

- I give you her telephone number, but I inform you that she has not given interviews for several years.

Robberta Close answered a call from Pedro Freire, from whom, incidentally, she was already waiting.

- Mr. Pedro Freire, I thank you for your interest in myself, but I decided a few years ago not to give any more interviews. It happened that some of them ended up being a reason for more demonstrations of discrimination and homophobic intolerance and what I want is respect and peace of mind.

- I suppose it hasn't happened with any Portuguese newspaper. In Portugal, people of your generation remember you with kindness.

- No, I have nothing to complain about either the Portuguese newspapers or the Swiss ones, which respect me. Unfortunately, they were some of the newspapers in my own country.

- If I send you by mail, clippings of all the articles that my newspaper has been publishing about LBGTI+, you will be able to verify the seriousness with which the subject is treated, from the perspective of a humanistic position in defending the rights of victims of discrimination and persecution, torture and even death, on a global scale.

When you realize our position in denouncing these reprehensible realities, I am convinced that you will want to collaborate in our campaign to defend LGBTI+ people.

I ask you, please read the articles. If after reading them, you maintain your refusal to give us an interview, I promise I won't bother you again. Can I send the items to you?

- I see that you are very persistent. Then, send me the articles and call me within three days to ask me where I stand on the matter.

- Thank you very much.

Pedro was already prepared in Switzerland with clippings of articles published by Expresso, all written by Laura and, for now, just one, his own. Everything was neatly presented in a file notebook he put in the mail. Three days later, as agreed, he called Roberta Close again.

- I have read the articles carefully and I can tell you that I intend to collaborate with your campaign

It turns out that we are not in Zurich at the moment. During holidays and many weekends, we are at our country house in the Alps. As I have always considered Portugal a friendly country for Brazilians, I am inviting you to come and spend the weekend at our house, so we can talk at ease. I'll send you the coordinates.

Pedro Freire rented a car to go from Zurich to the Swiss Alps. It is 120 kilometers to Chur, via the A3 and then along a secondary road until finding a typical mountain chalet, isolated in the landscape, overlooking the Rhine, on sloping land, covered in green pasture, punctuated in the distance by a large number of cows who wander, peacefully, through the mountain. A real Swiss postcard.

After a journey of about an hour and a half, through a landscape of dazzling beauty and serenity, Pedro came across a beautiful three-story wooden building.

Upon arrival, the couple welcomed him, toasting with Gluchwein, mulled wine with anise, orange and cinnamon, very typical in winter. May is already in full bloom, but in the mountains, it is still cold.

After being installed in a room with a view for the Rhine, Roberta made a point of showing the visitor around the house.

They quickly passed through the ground floor, which houses a spacious garage for three cars, two snowmobiles, and two kayaks, a sign that the hosts make good use of the environment.

In another room, there is a small snowplow tractor, the central compression engine for the air conditioning, as well as firewood for the fireplaces, and ski equipment.

The upper floor extends over an extensive terrace open to the outside, all made of wood, equipped with a barbecue, rustic wooden dining table.

Connecting the terrace to the interior of the house, a covered pavilion, fully glazed, houses a heated swimming pool, a heated hot tub and a small gym, well equipped with a variety of equipment, including a treadmill, stationary bike, rowing machine and body building equipment, justifying the excellent

physical shape that both members of the couple display.

Inside, it exudes luxury and sophistication. Wooden walls and ceilings, large windows benefiting the large room with generous natural light, a huge, lit fireplace gives a cozy atmosphere to the room, furnished with luxurious sofas, an exquisite Swarovski crystal chandelier, wonderful pieces of Murano glass decorate the rooms, shelves of an extensive library. A Van Gogh on the wall, which Pedro believes is an original.

On the same floor, as a complement to the huge kitchen, there is an extensive and well-organized wine cellar, housing perhaps two hundred bottles, from all over the world.

Upstairs, there are four bedrooms, all with private bathrooms. Two of them, face the mountain with the peaks still covered in snow and the other two, face the green meadows leading down to the Rhine.

Pedro was delighted with the house and the friendly way in which the couple welcomed him.

Whether Roberta or her husband are welcoming the Portuguese journalist with courtesy and affability as if he was an old friend or family member. Late Friday afternoon, they took a walk through the surrounding countryside, and passed by the small cottage attached to the main house, occupied by a Spanish couple, employees of the house, who share the cleaning, cooking, gardening and maintenance of facilities.

- As a rule, during the weekend, they don't work – Roberta informed – we are the ones who cook, but as we have visitors here, Consuelo insisted on coming to cook for our guest, but not tonight, because Roland intends to make a fondue.

- Does Pedro like fondue? - asked Roland.

- I confess that I have never eaten it but I will certainly like it. I like cheese a lot.

- Here at home, I'm the one who makes the fondue, I don't let Consuelo or Roberta do it, that's a Swiss thing. It's a small ritual, very much ours, that can even be done at the table.

- I also like cooking. Can I see how it's done?

- For sure. Let's go to the kitchen.

- The recipe is very simple and easy to make. No great culinary experience is required. The pan is very important. It has to be made of iron, so the cheese doesn't stick. The first thing to do is to rub a clove of garlic all over the inside of the pan, not only to add flavor, but to prevent the cheese from sticking to the bottom and burning.

Fondue is not the same across the country. Here in Eastern Switzerland, the cheeses we use are Appenzeller and Tilsiter.

In Roman Switzerland, the so-called Fondue Moitié-Moitié is made, with Gruyère and Vacherin Fribourgeois or Emmental.

Fondue Vaudoise is made with Gruyère and Fondue Valasiannel with Gruyère, Emmental and tomato pieces.

Roland threw 400 grams of one of the cheeses into the pan, still cold, and then 400 grams of the other, both grated. He added 4 deciliters of dry white wine.

He turned on one of the burners on the induction stove at medium temperature and slowly stirred the mixture until a homogeneous cream was obtained.

Then Roland added a little cornstarch, a cup of Kirsh and continued stirring the mixture. Finally, seasoned it to taste with salt, pepper and freshly shaved nutmeg.

He carried the pot to the table where was placed an alcohol lamp, which is to be kept lit during the meal, to keep the fondue warm and prevent it from curdling due to cooling.

Small pieces of bread, on the end of a skewer, are dipped into the very hot cheese and eaten, alternating with spring onions and pickled cucumbers.

To accompany the meal, white wine. Looking at the label on the bottle, Pedro was surprised.

- Swiss wine? I didn't know the country produces wine.

- Actually, Roland replied, few people know. We are known for our watches, benches, cheeses and chocolates, but practically no one knows that we produce wine of the highest quality. It's just that we drink all of it, the production is not very large.

Since most of the production takes place in mountain areas, on very steep slopes, which can be up to 90%, or on terraces, mechanization is not possible, which makes working in the vineyard difficult and increases production costs.

Therefore, our wine are not cheap at all, which would practically make exporting it impossible, even if there were a greater production.

A great wine lover, Roland revealed that he was an expert on the subject:

- We have 252 grape varieties, 80 of which are native. The most important and most widely planted of the native varieties is Chasselas. It produces delicate wines, with a certain subtlety, expressing aromas of white flowers, pear and lemon, with buttery and mineral notes. In Switzerland, there has even been a competition, exclusively for Chasselas, organized since 2012.

The next day, Pedro was treated to something different for breakfast from what he is used to eat in the morning. For him and Roland, the waitress had prepared Rosti, a crispy potato pancake, very similar to Spanish tortilla, with cheese, onion and bacon, accompanied by cold meats and chery tomatoes.

Roberta, certainly more concerned about her figure, prefers Birchermusli, a mix of cereals with pieces of apple, dried fruits, low fat yogurt and lemon juice.

As they had agreed the day before, the interview was scheduled for after breakfast on Saturday. Roland took the opportunity to go salmon fishing in the river.

- Roberta, can we start by talking about your childhood? Tell us about your family environment and when you discovered that you were different. And how did your family react?

- At the age of 11, even though I had a boy's body, I assumed my feminine identity and started wearing clothes that suited my condition. My family had a lot of difficulty accepting me, especially my father. He was very influenced by the opinions of his friends, which made him prejudiced, so he started telling everyone that I was the maid of the house.

The atmosphere at home became too tense, which led me to leave when I was only 14.

The atmosphere at school was not better. A teacher expelled me from school, which prevented me from finishing my formal education, but over time, I became self-taught and today I speak French, Italian, English and German.

I went to live with my grandmother who, although she didn't understand, she gave me all the support.

- I know you started modeling very early. Tell us how the change in your life began.

- I was 16 years old when one day, the famous singer and composer, Caetano Veloso drove past me in Rio de Janeiro. He came up to me, said he was impressed by my beauty and my height of 1.8 meters, and invited me to go to his agency.

It was true that at the time, I was very conspicuous and attracted a lot of attention wherever I went. Despite having a male identity document, the agency overlooked that because what they were interested in was beauty and elegance and there was no masculine trait in me, so I started taking part in fashion shows, first nationally, but later representing international brands such as Thierry Mugler, Guy Laroche and Jean Paul Gautier and being published in Vogue and Marie Claire magazines

At the age of 17, I was elected Miss Brazil Gay.

I was on the cover of the magazines Ele & Ela, Amiga, Contigo and Close, where my artistic name came from. I was on the cover of Brazilian Playboy and was the first transgender person in the world to be published in that magazine.

In the 1980s, I was already one of the most sought models in the world.

- We know that you also had an artistic career. What was that like?

- I started receiving invitations to act as a presenter on television. I took theater and music courses.

In the 1980s and 1990s, I was interviewed on the main television programs in Brazil.

- You also made films, didn't you?

- Yes, I did "No Rio Vale Tudo" in 1987 and also "O Escorpião Escarlate" in 1990.

I participated in soap operas on Manchete and Globo, but I suffered prejudice from several actors who refused to kiss me because of my gender identity.

I have been queen of the Rio Carnival, and paraded in the sambadrome for several years.

In 1998, I released the book "Roberta Close, Much Pleasure".

- I read something about being considered the most beautiful woman in Brazil.

- Yes, it's true, but not always for complimentary reasons, quite the opposite, to malevolently draw attention to my sexuality. The newspaper Notícias Populares wrote: "The most beautiful woman in Brazil is a man" and a North American newspaper wrote "The most beautiful model in the world is a man". Fame had its price to pay.

- When did you have gender reassignment surgery?

- It has been when I was 25 years old. It has been made in London and was a gift from a great friend of mine, which cost him a fortune.

- And continued in artistic life, until when?

- I stopped, definitively, in 1998, although I had already lived in Switzerland since 1993.

- When did you marry Roland?

- It was only after I had gender reassignment surgery and officially registered my identity as a woman, that I got married, I was then 29 years old. Since then, we have lived in Switzerland.

- Are you thinking about adopting a child?

- Roland was willing to do this, but I wasn't, and he respects my wishes.

- Do you have plans for the future?

- Above all, I want to lead a peaceful life, far from fame, and be respected, as I am, here in Switzerland, where I acquired citizenship and I am accepted as a woman integrated into Swiss high society.

As my last project, I am working on a biographical documentary, where I tell everything about my life, at the suggestion of an organization defending the rights of LBGTI+. If this can be useful to them, it costs me nothing.

- Do you intend to return to Brazil?

No. My family did not accept the marriage. At 57 years old, I don't want to feel the oppression of prejudices again. Here, I am a high society woman, everyone respects me. There, for many people, although I am successful, I am still nothing more than a transgender.

POLAND

2022

Lisbon and Sintra

On February 24th, the world was surprised by the news that the Russian Federation had invaded Ukraine.

Although tension in the region had been increasing since the Russians began large-scale military maneuvers in Belarus, an ally of Moscow, near the Ukrainian border, everyone, including Ukrainians, believed Putin's words when he assured them that these were just maneuvers and that there was no intention of invading Ukraine.

Although there were precedents in recent history, of the Russian Federation invading new countries that had been part of the Soviet Union, such as Chechnya, whose independence no one recognized, or supporting independence movements in Georgia and Moldova, no one expected Russian troops to invade Ukraine, despite having already done so in 1914, having then annexed Crimea as Russian territory, after a local referendum, which no one, apart from Moscow, recognized.

Apparently, it seemed that Putin believed that in a few days he would occupy Kiev and replace the government with some puppet under his command.

The intention of Ukraine joining NATO was unacceptable to Moscow, which saw this as a Western aggression and a threat to its security.

On the other hand, the intention was to reinforce the annexation of Crimea by integrating the entire Dombass region, annexed to Crimea, into the Russian Federation, which includes the pro-Russian separatist regions of Luhansk and Donetsk.

For domestic consumption, fueled by fully controlled information, and in a ridiculous attempt to throw dust in the eyes of the entire world, Putin justified the invasion not only to prevent future NATO aggression from

Ukraine, but also to free the Russophile Ukrainians from the neo-Nazi tyranny of the Kiev government, "a bunch of drug addicts and neo-Nazis".

Knowing that the President of Ukraine is Jewish, the accusation of Nazism was ridiculed worldwide, made worse when the Minister of Foreign Affairs of the Russian Federation, Sergei Lavrov, stated that the greatest Zionists had been Jews; in short, it was clear that the Holocaust had been caused   by   Jews!
A few days after the invasion, a Russian army column, 30 kilometers long, of military vehicles, armed vehicles and artillery, was paralyzed on its way to Kiev, due to logistical errors in fuel and food planning, in addition to the lack of motivation of recruits who had no idea where they were or what they were doing, and faced resistance from the Ukrainians, which they had not expected. Other realities that Putin did not count on were that the Ukrainian army was not the same, weakened, as in 2014, it was relatively well armed for close defense and well trained, just as he did not count on the resilience of the Ukrainians, who had already surprised the world in 2014, when they resisted barricades for 91 days, in the middle of winter, against cold and hunger and the violence of the police and the army, only giving up when the pro-Russian President Viktor Yanukovych gave up fighting the people and fled by helicopter to Russia. Neither Putin nor the Ukrainians themselves counted on the resilience of President Volodymyr Zelenskyy, a former comedian, from whom no one expected signs of leadership and patriotism, but who, from the beginning of the conflict, proved to be the cornerstone of resistance to the enemy and of attracting the support of many countries. Another thing Putin did not count on was that the invasion galvanized the union, not only of the countries of the European Union, but also of NATO, and of powers as far removed from the conflict as Japan, Australia and New Zealand, all willing to send money and weapons to fight the Russians. In reality, the conflict is between countries that defend freedoms and democracy and the autocratic neo-fascism that dominates the Russian Federation. Many accumulated errors in political analysis and in the strategy followed by Putin are resulting in the opposite of what he intended. By wanting to prevent Ukraine from joining NATO, Sweden and Finland, traditionally defenders of neutrality, fearing that they would become victims of Moscow's aggressive policy, they were forced to join NATO's mutual defense system.

The Russian invasion of Ukraine triggered an avalanche of refugees to neighboring countries, especially to Poland, but also to Slovakia, Hungary and Romania.

A wide range of actions to support refugees were immediately launched across Europe, whether through official initiatives by various governments or through private initiatives by non-governmental organizations, local authorities, firefighters and even individual civilians.

In Portugal, convoys of trucks loaded with winter clothes, blankets, food and medicine quickly formed. There were several individuals who loaded their car with the help of clothes and non-perishable food, heading to Poland, willing to bring families to Portugal.

The lawyer, Dr. Pamela, sensitive to the dramatic conditions of the refugees, decided to provide the help that was within her reach. Living alone in a mansion in the Serra de Sintra and enjoying a comfortable financial situation that she had inherited following her husband's death, she felt compelled to personally intervene, no matter how small her help might be, a small drop of water in the ocean of millions of refugees.

She decided to load the car with winter clothes and non-priceable foods, such as all types of preserves, chocolates, cheeses and milk for the children. He communicated his project to Katya Kovalenko, a Ukrainian she had met at ILGA, just as she was preparing to return to Ukraine. Katya lives in Lisbon and works as a nurse at CUF Hospital.

- But why do you want to go back to Ukraine at a time like this? And your job?

- I said goodbye to it, because I don't know how long I'll be there, or if I'll be back.

- But why now?

- For two reasons. Because my parents didn't want to leave my maternal grandmother who, due to her age and poor health, didn't agree to come to Portugal.

With the start of the war, I no longer had contact with them. We spoke two or three times a week and now the phone doesn't answer. I need to know what's happening to them. I only know that the village where they live was bombed, but I hope they are alive.

On the other hand, and regardless of what may have happened to my family, my intention is to go and participate in the war, as a nurse and as a combatant.

I will join the Kiev Valkyries, a female force of volunteer fighters, integrated in the Army, some of them doctors and nurses.

You will see a short video circulating on the Internet, addressed to Russian
troops. The motto is: "The Valkyries of Kiev will kill you".

In that case, if you want, I can give you a ride. If we're both driving, we'll get there faster.

2022

On the way to Poland

Pamela handed Katya a piece of paper where she had written down the itinerary for the trip to Poland.

- I created a travel plan for us to travel between 900 and 1,000 kilometers per day. If I were alone, I wouldn't be able to handle driving so long every day, but with both of us driving, we can take turns driving 200 to 300 kilometers and average 10 hours a day.

There will be no need to leave the highways to look for somewhere to sleep, because they all have hotels for travelers. To eat, we will always have restaurants at gas stations. Even so, without wasting time, I think we will only reach the border with Ukraine, on the fifth day of the trip. That is more than 4,000 kilometers.

- You are thinking about bringing refugees to Portugal. How are you going to prevent people from accusing you of promoting illegal immigration?

- Of course, I want to do everything officially. When we arrive, I will install them in my house, because I can afford it. The next day, I take them to the SEF, who will tell them what they must do to be admitted as war refugees.

If the refugee authorities are already able to receive them, I will deliver them wherever they tell me; if facilities are not yet organized to receive them, they can stay at my house until the authorities accommodate them, but meanwhile SEF will begin the official process of receiving them as refugees.

The first day's stage is to Zaragoza. Even Barcelona would be a bit exaggerated. There are 939 kilometers. Eight and a half hours are planned, plus stops to fill up with fuel, have a coffee, stretch the legs and have lunch. Let's count on more or less 10 hours of driving.

During the five days of the trip, there will be more than enough time and opportunity for the two travelers to get to know each other better, as their contact at ILGA had been superficial.

Talking, in addition to listening to some music, was still the best way to pass the time on a long journey.

- How long ago did you come to Portugal? – Pamela asked.

- I came in 2015, seven years ago.

- Why did you come?

- I need to explain to you what happened in my country, after 2014. I am from Crimea and worked in Sevastopol, at the Ukrainian Naval Forces Hospital.

In response to the popular victory in Maidam Square, in Kiev, when a demonstration that brought together a million people, did not move, for 91 days, in the middle of winter, in the cold and rain, faced unarmed, in improvised trenches, attacks by the police and even the army, and only ended when President Viktor Yanukovych fled to Moscow in a helicopter, Putin held a simulacrum of a referendum in Crimea, that concluded the desire of a Russian-speaking minority to achieve "reunification with Russia."

Since then, Crimea has been occupied by Russian troops and considered a part of Russia.

- Just like that?

- That is truth. Then they embarked on the Russification of the entire administrative apparatus. All public positions were occupied by Moscow supporters, the military intervened in everything, including the hospital where I worked.

I had no problems there for being an open lesbian because in Ukraine, since the fall of the Soviet Union, homosexuality has been legal, although some intolerance and sexual and verbal harassment persist.

The problem was that with the arrival of the Russians, the legislation changed: although, in the Russian Federation, homosexuality was decriminalized in 1993, in reality, homosexuals can be punished with fines, imprisonment, torture or corporal punishment, labor forced into concentration camps and even targeted for murder, as occurs in Chechnya, which is part of the Russian Federation.

So, I couldn't risk being subjected to any kind of persecution, I decided to go to Kharkiv, in free Ukraine, to find my parents, who took refuge there when the Russians occupied Crimea.

In any case, even though Ukrainian legislation is more tolerant towards homosexuals, marriage is not authorized between people of the same sex, not even in a stable union, just as the adoption of children is prohibited. At the time, a friend who had fled to Portugal, wrote to me and said that the Portuguese were very receptive to the arrival of Ukrainians, who are very welcoming and easy to find jobs, especially for nurses, of whom the country has a shortage, because nationals emigrated, especially to Great Britain, where they earn much more.

In Portugal you don't earn as well as in other European countries, but life is calm, the people is friendly, the food is good and the weather is almost always good.

It was then that I decided to go. I thought my parents could come to me later but they didn't accept, because they couldn't leave my maternal grandmother, who was too old to travel and change her life.

- How old is she?

- My grandmother Irina is already quite old, she is 94 years old, but she is not bad…for her age, anyway.

- So, she went through the 2nd war. There must be a lot to tell.

- Even worse than the war, that's what Ukraine went through in 1932 and 1933. Do you know what Holodonor was?

- I've never heard of it.

- Few people know but it was a crime of genocide perpetrated by Stalin, which Russia has always denied. There was a great famine throughout the Soviet Union and Ukraine, as had always been Russia's breadbasket, was taken by storm by the Party's political commissars, in charge of coercive collection from all farms, leaving farmers less than the minimum necessary to   survive. Condemned to produce to feed the Soviet Union and left with practically nothing to eat, many Ukrainians died of hunger and were buried under the snow, without their family members even having the strength to bury them. There were dead bodies everywhere.

United Nations estimated in 2003 reported between 3.3 and 7.5 million Ukrainian deaths due to famine, which was considered a genocide by 16 countries, always denied by Moscow, of course.

- How horrible!

- To survive, we ate anything and everything, from unearthed carcasses of dead animals, dogs and cats that disappeared, straw, tree roots, herbs, nettles, and all kinds of vermin, rats, snakes, frogs and even ants.

- How horrible!

- My grandmother told my mother, but she never wanted to talk about it again, she remembered when she was just five years old and both parents died of hunger, because they saved the meager crumbs they had for the survival of their three children, one day, she found it strange that they were eating meat, when no one had any, not even potatoes or wheat to make bread. In the absence of her parents, she was her older sister, then 12 years old, who was left to be the head of the family, consisting of the two of them and their seven-year-old brother.

One day, my grandmother decided to follow her sister, from a distance, to see where she was going to get food. She saw her blessing herself with the sign of the cross, as she passed the two crude crosses, improvised with two sticks crossed with wire, that marked hour parents' graves, buried in the snow.

Then she saw her approaching a neighbor's house, abandoned because everyone had already died.

She watched her dig through the snow until she found what she was looking for. With a knife, she removed a piece of meat and placed it in a bowl. She covered everything with snow again.

My grandmother said she returned home before her sister and never made the slightest comment about what she saw.

- The important thing is that the parents were respected – that was her only thought.

All three survived the Great Famine. If it hadn't been like that, I wouldn't have been born. I owe my life to them. So, I have to go.

2022

Ukraine War

The start of the Russian invasion of Ukraine triggered an avalanche of refugees who tried to reach the borders with European Union and NATO countries, especially Poland.

Since fuel became rationed and difficult to find, the limited supply of 10 liters, in reality, prevented any desire to travel, so many were forced to stay where they lived, left to their fate.

Public transport by bus, on roads still considered safe, was not enough for the crowds who wanted to escape the war.

Those who tried to escape towards Lviv and from there to Poland, on overcrowded trains, accumulated in the stations, until the Russians began to bomb them.

Those closest to the border took their cars until they ran out of fuel. Then, they abandoned the vehicles and continued on foot, along the road, taking with them, little more than what they had on their bodies, children and domestic animals.

Long lines of thousands of abandoned cars formed on the side of the road, while the human mole moved in silence, dragging with it desolation, tiredness and despair.

For many, their destroyed homes were left behind, everything they managed to achieve throughout their lives.

Wherever they went, the Russian armored vehicles systematically destroyed, one by one, all the houses, even the humblest ones, in tiny defenseless farming villages, without any military interest. The insane fury of destruction of civilian targets extended to schools, daycare centers, hospitals and even a maternity ward.

It is clear that it is Putin's policy to leave no stone unturned and destroy the soul of Ukraine, which according to him, is not a country, nor has a reason to exist.

His statements about his so-called "special military operation", which "is not a war, nor is it an invasion", and whoever says it is a war, is arrested for treason against the Russian homeland, which is intended to "liberate the Ukrainian people from the Nazi regime", are so ridiculous that one comes to doubt their mental state.

Once they arrived at the border, the men said goodbye to their wives, daughters and minor grandchildren and returned to their origins, where they had to present themselves, as all men between 18 and 60 could not leave the country.

At the border, only women, children, old people and domestic animals pass through, on their way to the unknown, nourishing an illusory hope of a quick return. No one, at the time, anticipated a prolonged war and everyone, in a way that surprised the world, placed hope in victory against the invader. With each passing day, the resilient and combative spirit of the people grew, fueled by the example of President Zelensky who surprised everyone, even those who had voted for him, who initially did not expect much from him who had been a comedian, with no connection to politics. and that, when he applied for the presidency and was asked the question of not having political experience, he replied that "it is not necessary to have political experience, what is needed is common sense".

When, on the third day of the war, the whole world thought that Russia would take Kiev by storm and replace Zelensky with a puppet government, the Americans rushed to try to save the President's life, offering him a helicopter to escape, to which he responded, in a way that made his position clear: "I don't want a ride, I want guns".

It was this lapidary phrase with which he solidified the confidence of Ukrainians and the support of free countries, the European Union, the United States, Canada, and even on the other side of the world, from countries such as Japan, Australia and New Zealand. Everyone agreed to support Ukraine with money and weapons and to sanction Russia with a series of economic measures and a boycott of its exports.

No one had ever gathered a consensus of support for an idea, on a global scale, like Zelensky, who through his combativeness and perseverance in defending the country, achieved something that no one had ever achieved, being heard in the National Assemblies of several countries, in the United Nations, in the European Union, in the G7, without leaving the country, and receiving support visits from leaders of several democratic nations.

In a short time, Zelensky had gone from being an unknown politician to being a hero recognized worldwide and trusted to defend not only Ukraine, but the free world.

Many nations have become convinced that if Putin is not defeated in Ukraine, the insanity of trying to recreate the Russian empire will be expected, starting with the invasion of Romania and the Baltic States, which would lead to a third and final world war, who knows, if the end of humanity, at least in the northern hemisphere.

The free world understood that the border between democracy and dictatorship is in Ukraine and that defending the country was defending the free world.

When least expected, the Russian military column on its way to Kiev reversed course, leaving behind a large number of vehicles and armored vehicles destroyed by artillery and ambushes by the Ukrainian army, in addition to a considerable number of vehicles and armored vehicles, abandoned without warning fight, due to lack of fuel or breakdowns, others, due to desertion of unmotivated and too young Russian soldiers.

As the Russian column retreated and changed its strategy, intending to concentrate the war effort in the Dombass region, leaving behind Kiev, and a trail of destruction in the small cities it had occupied, the war crimes that had been committed began to be discovered, from summary executions of men with their hands tied behind their backs, with a shot in the back of the head, to rapes.

There were families in which the only survivors were the girls who were raped and witnessed the murder of their family members, including children.

2022

Border of Ukraine

At the end of the fourth day of a long and tiring trip to Poland, Pamela and Katya arrived at night in the city of Lublin, where they spent the night and asked where is the closest place to the border with Ukraine, where there are already refugees.

They pointed out to them the small town of Korczowa, just 264 kilometers from Lublin and where Ukrainian trains arrive from Lviv, just 80 kilometers from the border and where thousands of refugees are passing daily. The next day, they left the hotel early, in order to reach their destination as early as possible.

Upon arrival, it was already the twelfth day of the war, they came across a human mass composed only of women, children and old people, all looking exhausted, silent and with an empty look, being assisted, with the possible organization, by entities such as the Red Cross and Doctors Without Borders, as well as other non-governmental organizations that provide temporary shelter to the new arrivals, clothes, coats and shoes for the winter that is still going on, hot food, water, milk and toys for children.

Reporters from television networks of several countries seek to interview people fleeing war, sharing dramatic stories that give an idea of the hell of destruction, fear and death they left behind.

Pamela's first concern was finding a place to unload the clothes and supplies she was carrying. There were several large tents set up for this purpose.

At Pamela's request, when they were still in Lisbon, Katya wrote in Ukrainian, a small text that was printed in large letters in A3 format, pasted on thick cardboard:

Bezkoshtovnyy transport from Lisabona, Portuhaliya, at 4 osoby, oplacheni vsi vytraty at proyizd.

Bizhentsyam z Ukrayiny zapevnyly ofitsiynu pidtrymku portuhal's 'koyi derzhavy.

In Portuguese, what Pamela asked to be translated was: Free transportation to Lisbon, Portugal for 4 people, with all travel expenses paid.

Official support from the Portuguese State provided to refugees from Ukraine.

Pamela asked Katya to accompany her, until she found someone to take with her, so she could speak to people who probably didn't speak English, only Ukrainian and perhaps Russian.

A young woman, accompanied by a girl, perhaps 10 years old, asked, in Ukrainian:

- You pass through Germany. Can you leave us there?

Katya translated and Pamela replied:

- No, sorry, I only take people to Portugal.

As the small poster that Pamela displayed attracted the attention of passersby, and because many had no idea where they were going next, what they wanted was to escape far away, to a safe place, far from the war, as quickly as possible, there was no shortage of interested parties surrounding the foreigner who was offering a ride.

- Please tell them that I give preference to at least one person who speaks English and, even better, if they have a driver's license.

Upon hearing Katya's translation, most people walked away, but there were still a few who asked questions:

- How many days of travel, what support does the Portuguese State have?

- Tell them that the Portuguese Council for Refugees provides for 18 months, housing and housing expenses, such as electricity, water and gas, subsidy for food, health in the public health service, which includes hospitals, teaching Portuguese, and job search, according to each person's qualifications.

They can be placed in several parts of the country, where there are conditions to receive them, and job opportunities, not just in Lisbon. At the end of the 18 months, to be able to stay in the country, you must already have a means of subsistence, a job or an activity started on your own.

The official reception of refugees takes a few days, but however long it takes, until housing is designated, you will stay in my house, which is very large and I am able to receive you. You don't have to worry about any expenses.

Of the few interested parties left, due to the need to speak English, only two young women remained, both in their late thirties. Either of them has a daughter, one of whom is 13 and the other is 15. Either of the two women had a driver's license, which would make the trip much easier.

Having been enlightened, the four Ukrainian women were invited to get into the car with their meager luggage.

Pamela said goodbye to Katya and thanked her for her help, wishing her luck on her brave adventure.

Pamela got on the path but, upon leaving the small town, she was stopped by a checkpoint. A Polish police officer and an individual in civilian clothes, wearing a large armband with a designation that Pamela could not translate but which featured a cross of Christ, approached the car.

The policeman said something in Polish, which Pamela implied she didn't understand and asked:

- Do you speak English?

It was the civilian who responded in good English:

- Where are you taking these people? They're Ukrainian, aren't they?

- Yes, they are Ukrainian refugees. I take them to Portugal.

- Can you show me an official document from your country that allows you to legally immigrate foreigners? Or are you a representative of an official refugee support organization?

- No. I just want to lend my particular support to refugees from the war in Ukraine, just as other individuals are doing, not only from Portugal, but also from other countries in Europe. I brought clothes and food, which I have already delivered, and I take refugees.

I intend to arrive in Lisbon and take them to the competent authorities to process the asylum request. Because I am a lawyer, I have a good understanding of the legal procedures on the subject.

- My lady, since you are not accredited by any official entity, you won't be able to take these people with you.

The man gestured to the police officer who ordered the four passengers to get out of the car.

- But why, what is happening? – Pamela asked, not understanding what was happening.

- I'll explain – replied the civilian. From the first days of the entry of refugees into Poland, mafiosi of various nationalities were discovered, who tried and some managed to take people, under the guise of humanitarian support, when in reality their goal is trafficking women and minors for prostitution or for organ trafficking.

Therefore, from now on, only official entities recognized as providing humanitarian support are authorized to transport refugees.

Surprised, but shaken by the situation, she replied:

- Very good, I'm glad you are controlling the situation, but I'm still shocked by the possibility of being mistaken for criminals.

- Understand, madam, that it has to be this way. We have to record your attempt to transport refugees, so I ask for your identification. It's just a formality.

Pamela handed him her passport.

The civilian opened his passport, looked surprised and showed it to the police officer, who also looked doubtful.

- Madam, it says here that you are a male.

The two Poles exchanged looks and the police officer implied that they had to take her to the police station to clarify the situation.

The doubt arose: could it be that the mafia was already sending seemingly harmless "women" to more easily attract refugees into prostitution? From criminals, you have to expect all kinds of Machiavellian strategies.

The two Ukrainian mothers, surprised by the explanations in English, which they heard from the civilian, that they understood, and above all, when they realized that Pamela, after all, was a man and whom they initially looked at with symmetry and gratitude, they began to look at her with disgust and with hatred, thanking the heavens for having been saved from the Satan in skirts.

At the police station, Pamela was told to wait while her passport was examined by the chief of police.

Pamela couldn't believe she found herself involved in such a serious misunderstanding.

Hours passed and no one appeared in the room to inform her of what they intended to do with her.

In the room, there were two large photographs hanging on the wall. One, from an individual who Pamela thought should be the President and the other, from someone much better known, the former Polish Pope John Paul II.

Knowing that Poland is a fervently Catholic country, it was even possible to understand that the civilian was from some religious order, on a fundamentalist mission to "police consciences".

Pamela couldn't help but feel outraged by the situation, which gave her food for thought.

On the one hand, the man who had already been considered a Saint by the Catholic Church while he was Pope, ignored the many complaints from victims of sexual abuse by clergy around the world. He hasn't done anything to stop this shame.

A man, who during his papal visits to the African countries most affected by AIDS and where there was hunger, instead of distributing millions of free condoms, preached against their use, because Jesus said "Grow and multiply".

In Pamela's thinking, instead of being sanctified, the man should have first been convicted at the International Criminal Court for crimes against humanity.

And now, with what morality and profound hypocrisy, is she subjected to the idea that she promotes the sexual exploitation of women and minors or organ trafficking?

Pamela spent a night in jail, given over to her silent revolt.

Only the next day, late in the afternoon, the same civilian who had taken her, went to the cell with a guard, released her, giving the explanation:

- We send your details to Europol to find out if you have any criminal records. There isn't, so you can go in peace.

He returned her passport, with an ironic and mocking air:

- Mr. Odacir Kauê Lencastre, have a good trip.